check va S }
change commentary

4 Maccabees

2¹⁴ change "stock bit"
to "stock element"

Change "Hell. Cross" to
"Hell. Rep" where appropriate
(ef 4⁽⁵⁻¹⁷⁾)

Guides to Apocrypha and Pseudepigrapha

Series Editor
Michael A. Knibb

4 MACCABEES

David A. deSilva

Sheffield
Academic Press

In memory of
William A. Strout,
'a righteous man made perfect',
and in honour of
Dorothy and Carl Snethkamp

Published by Sheffield Academic Press Ltd
Mansion House
19 Kingfield Road
Sheffield S11 9AS
England

Printed on acid-free paper in Great Britain
by The Cromwell Press
Melksham, Wiltshire

British Library Cataloguing in Publication Data

A catalogue record for this book is available
from the British Library

ISBN 1-85075-896-4

Contents

Preface

Perhaps few individuals set out to specialize in *4 Maccabees*, a text that has always remained outside the church's canon, yet still lurks about the fringes of certain Septuagint codices like an uninvited guest at a wedding reception. *4 Maccabees* was to be, for me, merely one among many comparative texts for a dissertation on the Epistle to the Hebrews (deSilva 1995a). After spending some time with the text, however, I could not help but be captivated by the author's ardour for the Torah and struggle to demonstrate its relevance and significance in terms that Hellenistic Jewish readers could appreciate. I could not help but be deeply engaged by the author's attempt to address an issue that frequently takes centre stage in the struggle to be truly human—the struggle to rise above emotions, passions, and sensations and to live out higher ideals of justice, courage, wisdom and temperance. Even though the apostolic witness sets forward an alternative solution to this problem (Gal. 5.13-25), I nevertheless honour the struggle of that Jewish author who found in his Scriptures the means for a life of virtue and the motivation for an enduring loyalty to the One God.

No scholarly work happens without much support and cooperation. I am indebted to Professor Michael Knibb for his thoughtful and careful guidance. I wish also to thank my colleagues at Ashland Theological Seminary, both administrators and faculty, for their support and encouragement. Finally, I wish to express my appreciation to Donna Jean, my wife, for her commitment to my engagements in research and writing that impinge so much on family time.

David A. deSilva
Ashland Theological Seminary
July 1997

Texts, Translations and Commentaries

Anderson, H., '4 Maccabees (First Century AD): A New Translation and Introduction', in J.H. Charlesworth (ed.), *The Old Testament Pseudepigrapha* (Garden City, NY: Doubleday, 1985) II: 531-64. Anderson provides a helpful general introduction to the book as well as notes which are an especially helpful guide to the textual variants among the versions.

Deissmann, A., 'Das vierte Makkabäerbuch', in *Die Apokryphen und Pseudepigraphen des Alten Testaments* (ed. E. Kautzsch; Hildesheim: Georg Olms, 1900) II: 149-76. The brief introduction and annotations have largely been superseded by more recent works.

Dupont-Sommer, A., *Le quatrième livre des Machabées* (Paris: Librairie Ancienne Honoré Champion, 1939). An early proponent of the later date for *4 Maccabees*, Dupont-Sommer's introduction is still quite valuable.

Grimm, C.L.W., *Viertes Buch der Maccabäer*, in *Kunzgefasstes exegetisches Handbuch zu den Apokryphen des Alten Testaments* (Leipzig, 1857): 283-370. The insights from this book have been largely culled by succeeding generations of scholars.

Hadas, Moses, *The Third and Fourth Books of Maccabees* (New York: Harper & Brothers, 1953). Hadas provides an extensive introduction to the text, together with major textual variants and annotations that are very useful for discovering parallel passages in philosophical and rabbinic literature.

Johnson, S.E., and John Breck, '4 Maccabees', in *The New Oxford Annotated Bible: New Revised Standard Version* (ed. B.M. Metzger and R.E. Murphy; New York: Oxford University Press, 1991). This modern translation is excellent, and the annotations in the *New Oxford Annotated Bible* are generally helpful aids for a first reader.

Klauck, H.-J., *4 Makkabäerbuch* (JSHRZ, 3.6; Gütersloh: Gerd Mohn, 1989a). A modern, critical introduction with annotations rich in comparative literature.

Rahlfs, A., *Septuaginta* (Stuttgart: Deutsche Bibelgesellschaft, 1935). This is the standard Greek edition, with complete listing of variants in codices Alexandrinus and Sinaiticus.

Swete, H.B., *The Old Testament in Greek* (Cambridge: Cambridge University Press, 1930) III: 729-62. The text presents Alexandrinus, and has been largely superseded by Rahlfs's critical edition.

Townshend, R.B., 'The Fourth Book of Maccabees', in *The Apocrypha and Pseudepigrapha of the Old Testament* (ed. R.H. Charles; Oxford: Clarendon Press, 1913) II: 653-85. Although dated, Townshend's introduction and annotations are still useful as guides to points of contact with Graeco-Roman, Jewish, and early Christian literature.

Abbreviations

AB	Anchor Bible Commentary Series
ABD	David Noel Freedman (ed.), *The Anchor Bible Dictionary* (New York: Doubleday, 1992)
AGJU	Arbeiten zur Geschichte des antiken Judentums und des Urchristentums
BZ	*Biblische Zeitschrift*
CBQ	*Catholic Biblical Quarterly*
EncJud	*Encyclopedia Judaica*
HTRDS	Harvard Theological Review Dissertation Series
JBL	*Journal of Biblical Literature*
JJS	*Journal of Jewish Studies*
JSHRZ	Jüdische Schriften aus hellenestisch-römischer Zeit
JSP	*Journal for the Study of the Pseudepigrapha*
LCL	Loeb Classical Library
LXX	Septuagint
OTP	James Charlesworth (ed.), *Old Testament Pseudepigrapha*
NTS	*New Testament Studies*
PG	J.-P. Migne (ed.), *Patrologia cursus completa … Series graeca* (166 vols.; Paris: Petit-Montrouge, 1857–83)
RAC	*Reallexikon für Antike und Christentum*
SBFLA	*Studii Biblici Franciscani Liber Annuus*
SJLA	Studies in Judaism and Late Antiquity
SBLDS	Society of Biblical Literature Dissertation Series
SVF	J. von Arnim (ed.), *Stoicorum veterum fragmenta* (4 vols.; Leipzig, 1903–24).
VC	*Vigiliae christianae*

1

INTRODUCTION

4 Maccabees represents the attempt by a pious Jew to make a continued commitment to the traditions of the ancestors, particularly the Torah, reasonable and even advantageous in the eyes of fellow Jews. It is a remarkable synthesis of Hellenistic philosophy and Jewish piety, which stands as a milestone in the ongoing task of reinterpreting tradition in the light of changing world-views and cultural environments. Rather than heaping up pious phrases from Jewish tradition that may have rung hollow in the ears of his audience, the author uses Greek rhetorical forms and philosophical ideas in order to make being Jewish in a thoroughly Hellenized world both tenable and sensible. In so doing, he does not compromise his ancestral faith, but rather gives it a new life and impetus.

The author returns to the period of the Hellenization crisis and the violent suppression of Jewish particularism, particularly as expressed in obedience to the Torah (175–164 BCE), which is known through such writings as 1 and 2 Maccabees. This time, however, it is not for the purpose of legitimating a dynasty of Jewish kings or promoting the observance of the festival of Hanukkah. His work focuses not on the military 'heroes' of the period, but rather on the no less heroic martyrs who endured brutal torture and execution rather than renounce their loyalty to the One God. He casts these martyrs as living examples of the Greek 'wise person', whose freedom and conscience no external compulsion can master. The author presents his work as a 'most philosophical' discussion of the thesis that 'devout reason is sovereign over the emotions' (1.1), for which the martyrs under Antiochus IV provide the most conclusive proof. *4 Maccabees*, however, is much more than a philosophical treatise. It presents an eloquent defence of the Jewish way of life as an honourable pursuit, leading to the perfection of those virtues that even Greek and Roman critics recognize to be indispensable. In this way, the

author encourages his hearers and readers to remain loyal to their ancestral law and to God, even in the face of hostile opposition from those
who regard Jews with suspicion and contempt.

The Author, Title and Date

Like all the other books of the Old Testament Apocrypha—with the
exception of Ben Sira—the identity of the author has not come down
to us. None of the Septuagint manuscripts containing the text in whole
or in part afford any hints of authorship. Eusebius (*History* 3.10.6)
attributed the book to Josephus, a tradition that was followed by
Jerome and led to the inclusion of *4 Maccabees* among later mediaeval
collections of Josephus's works. This suggestion, for which Eusebius
provides no explanation, is unconvincing. First, several technical points
tell against Josephan authorship (see Townshend 1913: 656-57;
Anderson 1985: 533): *4 Maccabees* makes several historical errors
avoided by Josephus (e.g. the fraternal, not filial, relationship between
Seleucus IV and Antiochus IV); Josephus uses Greek, declinable, forms
of Hebrew names, whereas *4 Maccabees* uses indeclinable transliterations
for most names; the florid style is quite unlike anything else in the
known corpus of Josephus's works; Josephus's own accounts of the
Hellenization crisis are impossible to reconcile with *4 Macc.* 3.20–4.26.
Even more telling, however, is the fundamental stance of *4 Maccabees*
that opposes accommodation to Gentile culture at the expense of
fidelity to the Jewish Law. Josephus can praise Joseph, the patriarch of
the Tobiad family that later supported the Hellenization of Jerusalem,
as 'an excellent and high-minded man' who 'brought the Jewish people
from poverty and a state of weakness to more splendid opportunities of
life' (*Ant.* 12.4.10 §224); such an author could not quickly turn to
praise those who died rather than compromise even in small matters to
the demands of the dominant Gentile culture. *4 Maccabees* praises those
who sacrifice everything for the sake of the Torah; Josephus's own
story is certainly not one of such unmixed dedication (so Townshend
1913: 657).

We must be satisfied, then, not to have a name for our author. We
can, however, see something of his character, education and commitments through the work itself. *4 Maccabees* is written not in the 'translation Greek' of a non-native speaker, but in flawless, even skilful,
Greek. The author possesses a high degree of facility with the language,
skilfully inventing many compound words and new forms of existing

words. His style indicates a much higher level of syntactical sophistication than most authors in the New Testament or Septuagint (seen, for
example, in his extensive use of the optative mood; Breitenstein 1978:
177-78). He uses precise rhetorical terms to describe his work, employs
categories of argumentation known from rhetorical treatises, ornaments
his discourse with a variety of rhetorical embellishments, and blends
together a number of identifiable rhetorical forms that are discussed, for
example, in the *Progymnasmata* (elementary exercises in rhetoric) of the
second-century Alexandrian rhetorician, Theon. Klauck (1989a: 665)
suggests that the quality of the language and structure is inexplicable
apart from the assumption of some formal training in rhetoric. J.W. van
Henten (1986: 146) speculates that the author was educated in the cus-
tomary fashion as an ephebe (that is, a young man enrolled in the gymnasium to receive the training of a Greek citizen). It is questionable,
however, whether the author was educated within the Greek ephebate:
his rhetorical skill, facility in Greek, and philosophical awareness might
well have been learned from Jewish masters, and his religious stance
certainly points away from a classical Greek education. Nevertheless,
the author was keenly attentive to the conventions and possibilities of
the rhetorical art of his period.

The author of *4 Maccabees* was clearly a devotee of Hellenistic philosophy. While it is no doubt correct to disavow any formal philosophical education or alignment with a particular philosophical school (for
Judaism *is* his philosophy), he nevertheless drew upon a wide range of
philosophical traditions, combining them skilfully to serve his purpose
and shaping them to accommodate traditional Jewish anthropology and
theology. Perhaps he did not possess a philosophical sophistication
beyond what would have been available to him as part of the common,
Hellenistic cultural heritage (so Klauck 1989a: 666), but he shows a
special interest in engaging, arranging and using the philosophical
material that was within his grasp. He was quite conversant with the
'philosophical *koinē*' of his time and had more than a passing acquain-
tance with Stoic and Platonic ethics.

His first commitment was, of course, to the One God and the
Jewish Torah given by that God to the children of Abraham. All his
rhetorical ability and philosophical interests served this higher loyalty
and were intended to promote this loyalty among his fellow Jews.
Living in a thoroughly Hellenized environment, he nevertheless
allowed no place for accommodation of the Torah to that environment, no mitigation of its requirements. Indeed, the Torah was for him

the teacher of the highest philosophy and the trainer of the cardinal virtues so prized by Stoics, Platonists and Peripatetics alike. The juxtaposition of the adjective 'devout' with the faculty of 'reason' throughout the work—with a clear emphasis on the importance of the adjective—exemplifies the author's basic interest in living as a faithful Jew and helping others do the same.

The original title, if there was one, has not come down to us in the usual appellative '*4 Maccabees*'. This title is rather misleading, because there is no mention at all of the actual Maccabaean family or the revolt they led. Rather, the book focuses on the martyrs who died under the persecution of Antiochus and the Hellenizing aristocracy prior to the first successes of their military compatriots. More appropriate, and probably more original, is the title given by Eusebius, namely, 'On the Supremacy of Reason' (so Anderson 1985: 532). This title follows the convention in antiquity of naming a treatise after its principle subject (e.g. Seneca's 'On Wrath', Dio's 'Concerning Distrust', Plutarch's 'On Exile', and the like).

We have no precise knowledge of when *4 Maccabees* was written. The author has most probably used 2 Maccabees directly, rather than borrowed from a common source (see 'Sources' below), and so it must be placed later than 100–90 BCE, the time at which 2 Maccabees was probably composed. The *terminus a quo* has been set later than this by Anderson (1985: 534), who notes that the explanation in 4.1 that the high priest was an office formerly held for life presupposes a situation in which the high priest no longer had life tenure, thus after 63 BCE. Elias Bickerman (1976a) has produced evidence that numerous scholars have regarded as solid and convincing. First, he notes that two Greek words are used (*thrēskeia*, 'religion', and *nomikos*, 'skilled in the law') that did not come into common use until the Roman period, specifically the reign of Augustus (30 BCE–14 CE). This moves the *terminus a quo* closer to the turn of the era. He further observes that Apollonius, the Seleucid-appointed administrator, is said to govern 'Syria, Phoenicia, and Cilicia' (4.2), which is a change from the description of his jurisdiction in 2 Macc. 3.5, where he is styled the 'governor of Coelesyria and Phoenicia'. Bickerman (1976a: 278) observes that Josephus also changed terms and political arrangements to reflect his contemporary situation, and so one may surmise that the author of *4 Maccabees* has changed his source for the same purpose. The linking of Syria, Cilicia and Phoenicia under the jurisdiction of a single administrator occurred only under Roman rule, from about 19 to 54 CE, thus giving a much

(72^{ab} — van Henten
1986 : 140 -)
142

narrower range of dates for the composition of the work. Bickerman (1976a: 280) suggests narrowing this down further to the period prior to the reign of Caligula, because there is no mention of the persecution against Jews under him, but this is a dubious argument from silence.

Not all scholars have accepted Bickerman's proposal. He has been rightly criticized for building on the alleged references in 4.20 and 14.9 to the Temple cult as extant—neither text bears out his claim that the Temple *must* still be standing. Neither does the opposite case (suggested by Breitenstein 1978: 171-74), that the partial omission of references to the Temple cult and sacrifices in *4 Maccabees* indicates that the Temple is no longer standing, carry any weight. As Collins (1983: 187) correctly observes, 'lack of interest in sacrifice is not surprising in a work written in the Diaspora'. Philo, long before the fall of the Temple, gave expression to a Judaism that could survive without a Temple. Klauck (1989a: 668) has also questioned Bickerman's conclusion concerning the significance of the linking of Syria, Phoenicia and Cilicia for the dating question. An inscription from 86 CE in which the three provinces 'Syria, Phoenicia and Cilicia' appear together suggests to him that the dates for speaking of these three as linked are not so clearly delimited to 19-54 CE. Moreover, J. van Henten (1986: 140-42) has shown that Cilicia was divided into two administrative jurisdictions and that the western region remained under the purview of the Roman governor of Syria until 72 CE (Suetonius, *Vespasian* 8.4). Nevertheless, the significant point is not the naming of these three together, but the placing of them under one *stratēgos* (Apollonius), reflecting a specific administrative arrangement of 19–72 CE (corrected in the light of van Henten's evidence), and so Bickerman's main thesis stands secure.

Dupont-Sommer (1939: 75-86), supported by Breitenstein, favours a later date toward the beginning of the reign of Hadrian (118–35 CE). He calls attention first to the stylistic similarities between *4 Maccabees* and the 'Second Sophistic', a renaissance of interest in classical philosophy that flourished toward the close of the first century CE. He suggests that the philosophical eclecticism in *4 Maccabees*, which has much in common with that of Dio Chrysostom, Plutarch and Epictetus, shows it to be the contemporary of these late first-century and early second-century philosophical writers. The 'Second Sophistic', however, was already popular under Nero, and R. Renehan (1972: 227) argues that a 'general eclectic tendency had come to characterize much philosophic thought' already by the first century BCE, such that one could speak of a 'philosophic *koinē*'. The author's eclectic use of philosophical ideas affords, therefore, no solid evidence for a later date.

Dupont-Sommer also drew out a number of parallels between the situation of the Maccabaean revolt and the unsuccessful Diaspora revolts under Trajan (115–17 CE), offering these as support for his view that *4 Maccabees* represents a response to the needs of Jews in the wake of these revolts. Granted that the Jewish resistance drained the Roman power sufficiently for Trajan to have to quit Parthia (as Antiochus met with defeat after his encounter with the Jews of Judaea), and that Trajan died on the way back to Rome (as Antiochus died away from home), it still must be admitted that Trajan did not proscribe the observance of Torah, that he did not become a persecutor of Jews, and that the martyrs executed by Antiochus were no armed revolutionaries. An author writing to encourage the Jews after their unsuccessful attempt at revolution could have chosen much more fitting subjects and epochs in Jewish history.

Breitenstein (1978: 177-78) finds evidence from his stylistic analysis of *4 Maccabees* to support a late date in the presence of signs of the later 'Atticizing' reaction to the florid, Asianic style that is characteristic of the work as a whole, but these signs are too weak to be at all decisive. More impressive, at first glance, is his statistical analysis of the vocabulary used by the author of *4 Maccabees* (1978: 13-29). First, Breitenstein clearly shows that the vocabulary of *4 Maccabees* is further removed than the New Testament and the Apostolic Fathers from the vocabulary of the Septuagint. Twenty-six percent of the words used by the author of *4 Maccabees* do not appear in either the canonical or apocryphal books of the Septuagint and *4 Maccabees* has especially close affinities with the vocabulary of the Wisdom of Solomon. This could be explained, however, by the author's proximity to philosophical and ethical discourse and to the Greek models that he emulates (for example, the Athenian funeral oration), and so offers little evidence for dating (except perhaps to strengthen the proposal that it was composed in the same period as the Wisdom of Solomon).

Secondly, Breitenstein investigates the connection between the vocabulary of *4 Maccabees* and non-Jewish literature of the Classical and Hellenistic periods and beyond. 4.67 per cent of the words used by the author of *4 Maccabees* are not attested elsewhere until after the turn of the era, 2.9 per cent of the words used by *4 Maccabees* are not attested elsewhere until the second century CE; 1.64 per cent are simply not attested elsewhere. From this evidence, Breitenstein suggests that *4 Maccabees* was composed around the turn of the first century CE. A closer examination of the words attested elsewhere only in second- and third-century texts reveals, however, that they are mostly compound forms or new grammatical forms of earlier existing words (such as the adverbial forms of adjectives and the like). Greek lends itself especially well to such variation and invention, evidenced in the 1.64 per cent of the author's vocabulary never found elsewhere, and does not demonstrate a late date. Most of the unique words can be accounted for by the author's inventiveness, which is already well-documented.

Van Henten (1986: 142-45) attempts to build on Breitenstein's argument for a date of composition around 100 CE. He contends that the author of *4 Maccabees* conceives of the 'fatherland' in a spiritual sense, and speaks of this as an indication of a post-70 CE date (after the fall of Jerusalem and the destruction of its Temple by the Roman army). Other authors in the Jewish Diaspora, however, are capable of even more intense spiritualizations of 'Jerusalem' and 'Zion' well before the fall of Jerusalem (e.g. Gal. 4.21-31; Phil. 3.20; possibly also Heb. 11.13-16; 13.11-14). He also argues against seeing in the alterations of historical details indications of the time of writing. He suggests, by way of *reductio ad absurdum*, that the naming of Seleucus as Nicator would suggest a date near either 281 BC or 95 BC (the two periods in which the reigning monarch was surnamed Nicator). Bickerman's rationale here, however, cannot be so easily dismissed, especially given the passages that he adduces from Josephus to demonstrate the tendency to read contemporary political arrangements into the narration of past events.

The similarities that van Henten recognizes between the pagan genres of the Athenian funeral oration, the narrations of the deaths of philosophers, the traditions of devotion to Roman generals, and the *Acts of the Alexandrian Martyrs* also do not provide support for a later date. While he correctly observes the patriotic tendency shared between Athenian funeral speeches (as early as the fifth century BCE), the *Acts of the Alexandrian Martyrs* (a work of Egyptian provenance celebrating native resistance against tyranny, in this instance the emperor Commodus in the late second century CE) and *4 Maccabees*, this merely demonstrates the longstanding tradition of praising those who die nobly for the honour and security of their city or nation.

Van Henten follows this with a comparison between *4 Maccabees* and Ignatius of Antioch concerning the self-understanding of the martyr. Both Ignatius and the Jewish martyrs place less value on this age than the next, and both share the idea that only through martyrdom can they validate their existence as Jews or Christians. Nevertheless, all this may still point to Ignatius's familiarity with *4 Maccabees* and certainly does not argue against an early date for the latter. That *4 Maccabees* has more in common with Christian martyr texts than pagan texts remains stronger support for the dependence of the Christian texts on *4 Maccabees* than for the hypothesis that both Jewish and Christian martyrologies arose together at the turn of the century.

Bickerman's thesis (as corrected by van Henten), though challenged by some, still provides the strongest starting point for dating this work. Given the points of contact between *4 Maccabees*, the New Testament documents, and the popularity of the book among the fathers of the early church (factors also acknowledged by Klauck [1989a: 669] to be important when considering the question of dating the work), a date in the first half of the first century CE appears most likely. Indeed, it is at this specific point of the question of 'influence' at which the matter of dating becomes most crucial. If future investigations yield evidence that tip the balance in favour of a later date, what is said below concerning the possible lines of influence between *4 Maccabees* and the texts of the early church will need to be rethought more in terms of points of contact, with *4 Maccabees* perhaps bearing witness to earlier traditions or concepts (much like the cautious use of rabbinic texts or *4 Ezra* and *2 Baruch* in New Testament study).

Location and Audience

The place of composition, like the author and date, is impossible to determine with certainty. Because much is known about the large Jewish community in Alexandria, and because Philo and other authors connected with Alexandria show an impressive awareness of Greek philosophical thought, there is always an urge to locate *4 Maccabees* there as well (Townshend 1913: 654; Grimm 1857: 293; Pfeiffer 1949: 215). There was hardly an urban centre in the Mediterranean world, however, that was not frequented by sophists and philosophers declaiming in the public places, and our author does not appear to have a more in-depth knowledge of Greek philosophy than could have been made available to his attentive ears through the orations and conversations in the market places and colonnades of any significant city. Indeed, the lack of allegorization in *4 Maccabees*, generally taken to be a characteristic at least of the Alexandrian tradition in which Philo stands, and which came to be associated with the early church writers of that city, argues against Alexandria. As Freudenthal (1869: 112-13) noted, Alexandria was not the only centre for Jewish literary production.

Many scholars have ruled out Palestine as a likely place of composition because of the author's skill in Greek rhetoric, his familiarity with Greek philosophy and, especially, his 'positive and purposeful use of it to argue the supremacy of the Law' (Anderson 1985: 534). It is certainly true, as Martin Hengel (1974 and 1980) has amply demonstrated, that the degree of Hellenization in Palestine should not be underestimated. Palestine was full of Hellenized urban centres. The 'mistake' in *4 Macc.* 4.20, placing the gymnasium *on* the acropolis of Jerusalem rather than below the acropolis, may point to a lack of familiarity with Jerusalem (and hence a non-Palestinian origin), but it also may reflect an intentional change of the source (2 Macc. 4.12) for heightened effect. Nevertheless, the need to promote Torah-observance using topics of Hellenistic philosophy does suggest a minority cultural environment (i.e. the Diaspora), in which Jews had begun to estimate value by the standards and terms employed by the members of the dominant culture.

Asia Minor and northern Syria have much to commend themselves as probable places of origin. E. Norden (1923: 416-20) argued that the work was composed in Asia Minor on the basis of the author's use of the ornate 'Asiatic' style associated with this region. Antioch, the Seleucid capital in northern Syria, is an attractive suggestion for a specific location (independent of the question of Antiochus's actual presence at the tortures [see *4 Macc.* 5.1], which may be a literary fiction). First, Antioch supported a very large, metropolitan Jewish community—one which was in a suitable place for appreciating the rhetorical polish and philosophical tenor of *4 Maccabees*. Secondly, Antioch was connected with the relics of the martyrs from a very early period. The Antiochene Jews cherished the memory of the mother and the seven sons, and their relics came to be venerated by the early church. Dupont-Sommer (1939: 67-68) lays great stress on the mention of the tomb in *4 Macc.* 17.8 and the proposal for an inscription in *4 Macc.* 17.9-10, regarding *4 Maccabees* as a graveside oration at the preferred site of the tomb of the martyrs. While this should not be taken as a definite indication of the occasion for the writing of *4 Maccabees*, the local interest in these martyrs makes Antioch a strong candidate for the place of composition.

In an early article (1986: 146-49), van Henten argued that the alterations made by the author of *4 Maccabees* to his source, 2 Maccabees, point to Asia Minor (specifically Cilicia) as the place of composition. In both 2 Macc. 3.3 and 4 Macc. 3.20, Seleucus is called the 'king of Asia', but 4 Maccabees adds the name Nicanor, which 2 Maccabees had used for a Syrian general, the anti-hero of the second half of his epic. As no known Seleucid monarch carried this name, however, van Henten prefers, on the evidence of the Syriac version, to correct the name to 'Nicator', a name carried by both Seleucus I and Seleucus VI. Secondly, 2 Maccabees does not specify the relationship between Seleucus IV and his successor Antiochus IV (who were in fact brothers), whereas 4 Macc. 4.15 labels the latter the son of the former. These two considerations point, for van Henten, to reminiscences of the reign of Seleucus VI Nicator (96/95 BCE) and his son Antiochus X, who was killed in an unsuccessful campaign against the Parthians. He posits that 4 Maccabees was written somewhere in the territory occupied by the Seleucid empire during these 'last convulsions' of its life.

These arguments are unconvincing for a number of reasons. First, the addition of the surname 'Nicanor' and the specification of the relationship between succeeding monarchs may merely reflect the attention to detail that is a part of the highly rhetorical and refined style of the work (which van Henten himself admits). Secondly, the 'alterations' are thought of as reminscences of events that took place 150 to 200 years before the composition of the work, and have bearing neither on the subject matter nor the contemporary situation of the author. Thirdly, 2 Maccabees already speaks of Antiochus IV's unsuccessful campaign against the Persians and his death in connection with that venture: a reminiscence of Antiochus X's death is not required to explain the mention in 4 Maccabees of the Persian campaign. Van Henten's use of alterations by the author of 4 Maccabees to 2 Maccabees is, therefore, not as convincing as Bickerman's use of the same.

A more recent investigation by van Henten (1994), on the other hand, has produced strong and solid evidence strengthening the proposal of Asia Minor as the place of composition. The formula that begins the literary epitaph for the martyrs in 17.9-10 (*entautha enkekēdeuntai*) resembles other Jewish funerary inscriptions found in Hierapolis and Eumeneia in Phrygia. A broader study of non-Jewish inscriptions shows that this formula is well attested throughout Asia Minor—specifically Ionia, Galatia, Lycaonia, Lycia and Phrygia—but less well attested elsewhere. 4 Maccabees, therefore, reflects the funerary inscriptions of these regions. He mentions the alteration in 4 Macc. 4.2, which introduces Cilicia into the jurisdiction of the Seleucid governor of Syria and Phoenicia, as most compatible with a place of composition in Cilicia.

4 Maccabees was written, therefore, in the Jewish Diaspora, most probably in an urban centre with a significant Jewish community somewhere in Syria or Cilicia. This audience would have welcomed the exhortation to remain loyal to the Torah, but needed to see that Torah-observance led to a life that could be understood as virtuous and honourable even by Greek ethical standards, even if the religious differences would never permit *rapprochement* between the two cultures. Antioch remains an attractive suggestion, all the more as its centrality to the early church would more easily explain the use of *4 Maccabees* by Christians during the first four centuries CE, but other cities in Phrygia, Lycia and Lycaonia would also have a strong claim to consideration.

4 Maccabees clearly and explicitly addresses Jews. While the opening lines may read like an open defence of a philosophical proposition, or even serve as a defence of Judaism before a Gentile audience, the conclusion reveals unmistakably the intended audience: 'O Israelite children, offspring of the seed of Abraham, obey this law and exercise piety in every way' (18.1). Unless the author was a poor judge of his audience, the form and style of the work may reveal something more about these particular Jews. The Jewish community he addressed (or, at least, a significant part) possessed a certain literary sophistication and valued the claim to philosophical status (so Collins 1983: 191), that is, it possessed a notable intellectual element. These Jews were sufficiently Hellenized to require, or at least find useful and enjoyable, a demonstration that the Jewish way of life was compatible with the highest goals of Greek philosophy. They would remain fully dedicated to their ancestral religion not by living in an isolated ghetto, but by reassuring themselves that the Torah was a superior trainer in virtue and nobility than the Greek way of life.

Occasion

Various proposals have been made concerning the occasion for this discourse. Some scholars have questioned whether it was composed for actual oral delivery, or whether its apparent 'oral' elements are part of a literary fiction. The opening fulfils perfectly the aim of the rhetorical *exordium*, namely rendering the hearers docile, benevolent and attentive. The author urges the audience directly to pay attention to the philosophy that he is about to expound (1.1b). The discourse gives two clues that it is a speech composed for delivery at a specific event (1.10,

'on this anniversary'; 3.19, 'the present occasion'). The author even
speaks directly of the immediate effect of his speech on author and
audience alike (14.9: 'even now, we ourselves shudder as we hear of
the suffering of these young men'). The frequent use of imperatives
(e.g. 14.11, 13; 16.5) and forms of direct address (18.1) heighten this
sense of actual delivery. M. Gilbert (1984a: 316-19) and Dupont-
Sommer (1939: 67-73) take these clues as decisive evidence that the
discourse was composed for actual delivery, but all these factors could
equally well contribute to the literary fiction of producing an actual
speech, and it is impossible to decide this question with any degree of
certainty. There are no indications that the discourse could not have
been delivered (*pace* Breitenstein), and one would assume that the
author, even of a fictive discourse, presumed an actual audience in
some form. Indeed, Deissmann (1900: 151) argued that, while it may
well have been delivered before an audience, it was intended to have a
wider circulation and so was disseminated as a tractate, a 'book in the
form of a speech'.

What might have provided the occasion for the composition and
delivery of *4 Maccabees*? Some critics (Freudenthal 1869: 105; Thyen
1955: 13) suggest that it was composed as a synagogue sermon. The
objection is often raised that synagogue sermons took a scriptural text
as their starting point and were devoted to expounding the significance
of that excerpt. Townshend (1913: 653) rightly notes that we know
too little about the synagogue preaching of the first century to be able
to make any final rulings. While Jesus in the synagogue of Nazareth
commented (however briefly) on the passage he read (Lk. 4.16-30), it
is not altogether clear how Paul's 'word of exhortation' in Acts 13.16-
41 is limited to an exposition of the reading of the 'law and the
prophets' that came before (13.15). It is also objected that the philosophical tone of *4 Maccabees* precludes its use in the synagogue, but here
again Townshend's caution holds good. Dupont-Sommer (1939: 25)
suggested that some variety in preaching style within the synagogue
should be expected in view of the Hellenistic-Jewish adaptations of so
many literary forms in the written texts that have come down to us. *4
Maccabees*, with its ultimate dedication to the One God of Israel and
that God's Torah, would be no less at home in the synagogue than in
the lecture hall (so Anderson 1985: 536).

The difficulty with placing the work within the framework of a typical synagogue service, together with the indications within the text of
a more specific occasion (1.10; 3.19), have led a number of scholars

(Amir 1971: 662; Hadas 1953: 103-105; Dupont-Sommer 1939: 67-73; S.K. Williams 1975: 174-75) to suggest that *4 Maccabees* was composed as a commemorative address for the celebration of the anniversary of the martyrdoms. Hadas (1953: 103) and Amir (1971: 662) suggest delivery at the supposed site of the tombs of the martyrs (over which a synagogue appears to have been erected soon after the destruction of the Jerusalem Temple; see Schatkin 1974: 103). The form of the speech (see 'Structure and Form' below) would be quite appropriate to such an occasion because ancient commemorative addresses often combined praise for the fallen with exhortations to the living to follow the same noble course. Nevertheless, one should not assume that this form necessitates oral delivery at such a commemorative festival. Van Henten (1994: 47) points to two other funeral orations (Plato, *Meno*; Lysias, *Oration 2*) which show that *4 Maccabees* may be a strictly literary work not intended for oral enactment.

Rabbinic Judaism does not support any cult of the dead, but some honouring of the tombs of the dead is not entirely without precedent in Judaism. Hadas (1953: 106-107) notes the existence of an annual fast commemorating the death of Gedaliah, who saved Jeremiah's life, as well as the tradition documented in Rashi's comment on *b. Yeb.* 122a, where he speaks of disciples and others sitting around the grave of a teacher to honour him on the anniversary of his death. Moreover, a Jewish community that had been sufficiently Hellenized might have adopted the Greek custom (later more vigorously rejected) of honouring dead heroes annually. Such an occasion would also explain why the author limits his subject to the martyrs themselves without any reference to the victorious Hasmonaeans (S.K. Williams 1975: 175). Nevertheless, this suggestion remains problematic—not least of all on account of the lack of explicitly Jewish commemoration of these martyrs. There is need for caution in reading early Christian observances back into the Jewish community, and other reasons may account for the author's silence about the family of Judas Maccabeus.

An alternative suggestion for the specific day (1.10) and season (3.19) envisioned by the discourse is the Feast of Dedication, or Hanukkah, which is possibly more appropriate than a festival commemorating the martyrs that is otherwise unattested in Jewish sources. Hanukkah is traditionally linked with the liberation and purification of the Jerusalem Temple by Judas Maccabeus and his forces. The martyrdoms celebrated in *4 Maccabees* occurred during the Hellenization crisis that Judas, in effect, ended, and so the celebration of the restoration of Judaism in

Israel might also recommend some remembrance of those who died
during the oppression (and indeed these martyrs appear prominently in
2 Maccabees, the document promulgating most vigorously the observance of this new festival).

A frequently raised objection to this view is that *4 Maccabees* includes
no reference at all to the military heroes of the Hasmonean family, or
their victory over Antiochus's forces, which would more properly have
occupied centre stage during Hanukkah. Townshend (1913: 667), sens-
ing this difficulty, argues that there are allusions to the military heroes
in *4 Macc.* 1.11 and 18.4, but apart from the fact that both references
are debatable, they would provide such minor and indirect coverage of
the Hasmonean family's achievements as to be negligible. The basic
claim that Hanukkah must somehow focus on the exploits of Judas and
his brothers, however, may itself be open to question. Lingering disaf-
fection with the Hasmonaean dynasty (particularly its later representatives) among parties in Palestine might have discouraged many Jewish
communities from celebrating Hanukkah in such a way as to continue
to legitimate, in effect, a rule that was now regarded with mixed feelings at best. A Diaspora community, moreover, would have had greater
distance from a line of Palestinian kings—let alone one regarded with
such mixed feelings—and could have sought more meaningful heroes
for the celebration of Judaea's deliverance.

Any mention of the military exploits of Judas and his brothers
would, moreover, run counter to the author's own interpretation of
that crisis. It was the martyrs, not the warriors, who defeated the tyrant
and compelled him to leave the land (1.11; 17.20-22; 18.4-5). This
author shares with 2 Maccabees the view that the sacrifice of the righteous for the sake of the Torah was essential for the liberation of Israel
from Antiochus's armies, for it was the martyrs who turned away God's
wrath and secured God's renewed favour and deliverance (4.19-21;
6.27-29; 17.21-22; cf. 2 Macc. 4.13-17; 5.17-20; 6.12-17; 7.32-33,
37-38; 8.5). The faithful martyrs become, therefore, the essential
heroes of the Hellenization crisis, whose deaths set the wheels of victory in motion. Particularly in the Diaspora, the martyrs' resistance and
fidelity might be much more appropriate and accessible than the resistance to Hellenization through military uprising.

Hanukkah remains, therefore, a fitting occasion for such a 'narrative
demonstration' of fidelity to the Torah and to the patron–client bond
between God and the Jewish people. A second, though perhaps less
appropriate, occasion might be one of the festivals focused on the giv-

ing of the Torah, such as the Feast of Weeks (Pentecost) or Simḥat Torah (the 'Joy of the Law', the ninth day of the Feast of Booths). The protreptic thrust of *4 Maccabees* is that the Torah ought to be kept as the surest, and only perfect, path to virtue and eternal honour, no matter what the cost in terms of life in a Gentile-dominated world (cf. 18.1-2). The choice of martyrs as examples is not as inappropriate to these festivals as it may seem at first: a day to celebrate the Torah and the virtues of following its way of life would be a suitable occasion to speak of those who died rather than abandon that way of life.

Of the various proposals discussed above, Hanukkah remains perhaps the strongest possibility if one must opt for a single choice. Klauck's view (1989a: 664) is surely more to the point, however: namely that *4 Maccabees* addresses the 'everyday situation' of Diaspora Judaism, where the leading problem, with which the author is wrestling, is assimilation. I shall look more closely at this situation, and at the purpose of *4 Maccabees* within that situation, in the next chapter.

Structure and Form

4 Maccabees is rather clearly divided into two parts. The first, and shorter, part is the philosophical discourse that comprises 1.1-3.18. *4 Macc.* 1.1-12 provides the *exordium* that introduces the thesis and the method of demonstration; 1.13–30a 'defines' the philosophical terms; 1.30b–3.18 supply specific examples from Israel's law and sacred history of the truth of the philosophical proposition. The second, and longer, part takes up the 'narrative demonstration' of the thesis through the recounting of the martyrdoms. *4 Macc.* 3.19–4.26 provides as briefly as possible the historical setting of the martyrdoms; 5.1–7.23 describes the martyrdom of the aged Eleazar, relates this narrative back to the philosophical thesis, and offers an encomium in praise of the martyred priest; 8.1–14.10 follows the same threefold movement with regard to the martyrdoms of the seven brothers; 14.11–17.6 follows the same movement as it considers the suffering and death of the mother of the seven. *4 Macc.* 17.7–18.24 forms a peroration to the whole, celebrating the martyrs' achievements and commending their way of life for the audience's imitation. Scholars are in essential agreement about the structure of the discourse, although they differ markedly on the relationship between the two parts. Breitenstein (1978: 148-51) and Dupont-Sommer (1939: 19), for example, regard the two parts as loosely if at all related to one another

(Dupont-Sommer even suggests, tentatively, multiple authorship); Klauck (1989a: 648) and P.D. Redditt (1983: 262-63), on the other hand, understand the two parts as closely connected and mutually informing. There is, indeed, little ground for doubting the connectedness of the two parts, as the author does in fact unfold the whole work exactly as he discloses in 1.7-12, both with regard to content and style (i.e. demonstration side by side with panegyric).

What sort of literature is *4 Maccabees*? A document's genre, or literary form, and purpose are integrally related. The attempt to determine the genre of a work, therefore, is more than the search for a label—it is the search for its author's purpose and the work's intended effect. Many literary descriptions of *4 Maccabees* have been offered: diatribe, commemorative speech (eulogy, *epitaphios logos*), panegyric (encomium), synagogue sermon, lecture. The first two categories appear to be the most instructive and fitting for an analysis of *4 Maccabees* (van Henten 1993: 121). The book certainly belongs to the rhetorical genre called 'epideictic', or demonstrative, oratory. This category is the least well-defined, and, indeed, became a sort of catch-all category for speeches that were not clearly deliberative (advisory) or forensic (judicial). The author's own language points to this category: he uses the language of demonstration (*epideiknusthai*, 1.1; *apodeixis*, 3.19; *apedeixa*, 16.2), which matches his concern to demonstrate a philosophical proposition, stated conspicuously at the outset; he also uses the language of praise, appropriate for a funeral oration, commemorative speech, or simply a piece of moral exhortation (*epainos*, 1.2; *epainein*, 1.10). Indeed, the most promising course appears to be to understand *4 Maccabees* as a mixture of several forms serving a particular goal.

First, *4 Maccabees* may be compared to the 'diatribe'. As a philosophical discourse that begins with a discussion of a philosophical principle and then expounds that principle through several examples, the first three chapters of *4 Maccabees* share much in common with, for example, the discourses of Epictetus. It would be a mistake, however, to leave the discussion of the form of *4 Maccabees* at this initial observation, for it might also lead one to suspect that its primary purpose was merely the demonstration of a philosophical principle. J.C.H. Lebram (1974: 82-83) has rightly noted that the second part of the book is hardly adequately described as examples tacked on to a philosophical discourse in order to prove a thesis. The philosopher's use of an example is usually limited to brief recounting of the salient points and is indeed much like what one finds in 1.30b–3.18. The extended encomiastic reflections on the martyrs as exemplars goes beyond the diatribe (even though Seneca's *De constantia* goes further in this direction as he recalls the praiseworthy examples of Cato Minor and Stilbo). Lebram (1974: 82) overstates the case that the examples are not related to the philosophical thesis of 1.1–3.18, to be sure, but his overstatement serves as an important reminder that the *encomium* aspect should be taken as seriously as the demonstration (*epideixis*)—what is really at stake for this author is not the philosophical thesis, but the lifestyle defended by the martyr–heroes.

Lebram's own suggestion (1974: 96) for the literary genre (at least of the second part of *4 Maccabees*) is the *epitaphios logos*, the funeral speech for the dead consisting of a narrative that recounts the basis for the praise of the dead, the praise itself, and encouragement to the living (comprising consolation, dirge and exhortation). *4 Macc.* 3.20–18.24 contains all these elements. Other typical elements of the Greek 'epitaph' appear in *4 Maccabees* as well, notably the exhortation to the hearers to hold fast to their laws rather than submit to a tyrant and the emphasis on the temporary nature of life and the eternal value of the rewards to be gained by virtue and valour. (*Redo it*)

4 Maccabees shares much in common with ancient funeral orations or commemorative speeches. Such speeches set out to praise some figure by showing him or her to be the exemplar of a specific virtue or cluster of virtues. The speech was meant not only to honour the dead, but to promote the imitation of those virtues by the living—indeed, ancient orators knew that the praise of the dead would only be believed and accepted to the extent that the hearers could imitate their virtue and attain an honourable remembrance themselves. Funerary speeches often concluded with direct exhortations to fix one's gaze upon the noble life just praised, and to set as one's goal the embodiment of the same virtues in a way appropriate to one's sphere of life (see, for example, Thucydides, *Histories* 2.43-44; Dio Chrysostom, *Orations* 29.21). Our author also concludes with an exhortation to imitate the martyrs' dedication to the Torah (18.1).

Nevertheless, the oration is in fact framed as a philosophical demonstration of a thesis (1.1, 13, etc.), of which the martyrs are the best proofs (1.7-9). A strong mixture of philosophical argument and encomiastic reflection on specific individuals' lives is not without parallel in the first century CE. Seneca, the Stoic author and tutor to Nero, wrote a treatise called 'That the Wise Man Receives Neither Injury nor Insult'

(*De constantia sapientis*), in which he presented numerous arguments for his thesis, but depended most heavily on the examples of Cato the Younger and Stilbo of Megara, who showed how the philosophy was effective in life situations. The recollection of their particular triumphs over injury and degradation through holding to Stoic philosophy was aimed explicitly at making that philosophy all the more appealing to Seneca's readership.

Perhaps the best way to describe *4 Maccabees*, then, is as a sort of 'protreptic' discourse similar to Epictetus's discourse on the true Cynic (*Discourses* 3.22)—an oration that mingles philosophical argumentation and vivid examples of the philosophy at work, all for the purpose of making that philosophy more credible (cf. *4 Macc.* 7.9), appealing and worth wholehearted commitment. Such a work is not necessarily an invitation to outsiders to join the 'way of life' outlined by the philosophy: those who had already started along such a road (or had been born into that 'way of life', as were Jews) needed frequent encouragement to persevere, particularly when the dominant culture did not accept such a way of life as honourable or reasonable (cf. 5.7-11). *4 Maccabees* seeks to strengthen the commitment of Jews to the Jewish way of life, making that way of life credible, reasonable and honourable through the double presentation of argument and example.

Sources, Integrity, Text and Transmission

The author clearly drew inspiration from the Septuagint, the Greek translation of the Hebrew Scriptures. The first three chapters make frequent reference to dietary and social laws found throughout the Pentateuch, as well as to episodes and events from Israel's sacred history. The second part contains numerous references to the examples of Isaac, Daniel and his three companions, as well as several direct quotations from the Septuagint. It is indeed striking (and no doubt in keeping with his purpose of showing that 'children of the Hebrews alone are invincible where virtue is concerned', 9.18) that this author draws all of his examples from the Jewish Scriptures, whereas even Philo could draw on the stock of Greek and Roman worthies to illustrate his points.

Many scholars have been impressed by the similarities between 2 Maccabees 3–7 and *4 Maccabees*, concluding that the author of *4 Maccabees* has expanded the incidents recorded in those five chapters of the earlier work into the primary subject for his discourse. Klauck

(1989a: 654) has laid out these similarities in a convenient table:

2 Maccabees	4 Maccabees	
2.32	3.19	introduction
3.1-3	3.20-21	favourable situation under Seleucus
3.4-7	4.1-4	Simon's threat to the peace of the Temple
3.8-40	4.5-14	frustration of the temple-robbery
4.7-17	4.15-20	change of government; Jason as high priest
5.1-26	4.21-23	conquest and occupation of Jerusalem
6.1-11	4.24-26	coercive measures under Antiochus
6.18-31	5.1-7.23	martyrdom of Eleazar
7.1-41	8.1-17.6	martyrdom of the seven brothers and their mother

This close parallelism leads naturally to the hypothesis that *4 Maccabees* used *2 Maccabees*. The differences between the two books are, indeed, quite marked. For example, *4 Maccabees* writes the character of Heliodorus completely out of the history, and attributes to Apollonius the actions of three distinct characters in 2 Maccabees. Such departures from 2 Maccabees led Freudenthal (1869: 72-90) very early in the history of investigation to propose that both 2 Maccabees and *4 Maccabees* used a common source (the lost history by Jason of Cyrene mentioned in 2 Macc. 2.23), and that their different interpretations of, and interests in, that source account for the differences between them. Apart from the difficulty of testing such a theory (since the posited source document has not survived), this hypothesis becomes unnecessary when one considers the purpose of *4 Maccabees* and the use of 'historical' narrative (*diēgēsis*) in classical rhetoric.

The *diēgēsis* is defined by the second-century Alexandrian rhetorician Theon as a 'discourse expository of things that happened or might have happened', and different degrees of historical truth claims adhered to different historiographical writings: the 'true history' (*alēthēs historia*), the 'false history' (*pseudēs historia*), and the narrative that preserves some basic history while departing from exact history in order to present some trans-historical truth (*hōs alēthēs historia* or *plasma*)—the sort of poetical truth that Aristotle regarded as truer than exact history (*Poetics* 1451b5-10). A historical event serves as the basis and setting for a demonstration of a more ethical nature. This is precisely what one finds in *4 Maccabees*. A historical episode is being reconsidered not for the sake of providing a 'true history' of what events happened in exactly what order (claims made, for example, by Luke in his prologue, 1.1-4); rather, the author's goal is to demonstrate from reflection upon these events the sort of 'universal' truth that Aristotle classifies as the province of poetry, not history. *4 Maccabees* has abridged the historical backdrop of the Hellenizing crisis to a bare minimum—just enough to provide an adequate setting for the martyrdoms. Three and a half chapters in 2 Maccabees are thus trimmed down to twenty-eight verses in *4 Maccabees*. Conflating characters and ignoring many developments was necessary so that the author could arrive at his subject briefly without wearying his audience. Changes in detail, such as the descriptions of the tortures, stem from the author's inventiveness and the literary conventions of the period, where artistic embellishments served to promote the ethical goal of the narrative. The author's freedom in handling even a biblical story (David's thirst in 2 Sam. 23.13-17// 1 Chron. 11.15-19; cf. *4 Macc.* 3.6-16) should alert us to the considerable latitude he enjoyed with his sources.

The unity of the work has been challenged on several points. The opening paragraph has been subjected to rigorous criticism: Freudenthal (1869: 148-55) and Dupont-Sommer excise 1.3-4 as a clumsy attempt by a later copyist to reconstruct a damaged text by culling ideas and words from the first three chapters; Deissmann (1900: 151), Freudenthal (1869: 150-52) and Dupont-Sommer (1939: 88-89) agree that 1.5-6 (which substantially covers the same ground as 2.24-3.3) is either an interpolation or, at least, out of place in its present context. *4 Macc.* 1.3-4, however, prepares for what follows very well, extending the claim made for 'devout reason' as the path to prudence in 1.2 to include the other three cardinal virtues as well (justice, courage, self-control). The author develops this through 1.30a–2.23, restates the thesis in 5.22-24, and, indeed, presents the martyrs throughout the 'narrative demonstration' as exemplars of courage, justice and wise choices. 1.3-4 is therefore integral to the task of the *exordium* (the introduction of a speech). Similarly, 1.5-6 introduces briefly what is developed at greater length in 2.24-3.18, and so may claim a place in the *exordium*.

Although it is striking to find an objection to opposing points of view already in 1.5-6, Klauck (1989a: 686; 1989b) has rightly shown that it was the proper function of an *exordium* to create distance between one's hearers and the point of view against which one argues and to prevent misunderstandings of the speaker's point. *4 Macc.* 1.5-6 could serve either end. Another explanation for the form of 1.5-6 (i.e. an objection) may be found in the rules for the development of a *chreia* (an elaboration or a brief retelling of a person's wise or witty response, either in speech or deeds; see Hock and O'Neil 1986: 174-77), wherein a thesis is presented with some praise for the subject, restated in an expanded form, and then stated a third time 'from the contrary'. This is an exercise performed as part of the elementary studies for rhetoric. *4 Macc.* 1.1-6 follows this pattern admirably: 1.1-2 offers the thesis (no longer a saying of a famous person, but rather a philosophical topic) with a brief word of praise for the value of the subject; 1.3-4 restates the thesis in an expanded form; 1.5-6 restates the thesis (found in v. 6a) from the contrary position. There are, therefore, good reasons for accepting the opening paragraph as original.

The conclusion of the discourse has also received much attention from those who question the unity of *4 Maccabees*. Dupont-Sommer (1939: 152) has suggested that the original peroration need have contained nothing more than 17.7-22 with 18.20-24; L. Rost (1971: 81), Freudenthal (1869: 155-56) and Deissmann (1900: 175) agree that 18.6-19, a second speech given to the mother, fits poorly in its present context. Freudenthal would reject this passage as original on the grounds of the alleged inferiority of its Greek, its propensity to cite the Jewish Scriptures, and the author's lack of interest elsewhere in domestic life. Deissmann has rightly objected to the first two criticisms, noting that the language is not inferior, and that the first part of the discourse incorporates many specific references to the Scriptures, as well as allusions to the stories of Isaac, Daniel and his three companions throughout the martyr narratives (which appear again in 18.6-19). While Deissmann suggests inserting 18.6-19 into the mother's earlier speech in 16.16-23, it seems best left where it stands. First, it is not unknown for a commemorative address for fallen heroes to end with some words addressing female virtue. Pericles' Funeral Oration (in Thucydides, *Histories* 2.35-44), for example, concludes the praise of the fallen Athenian soldiers with a few words of exhortation to Athenian women, urging them to remain out of male spaces and the public eye (somewhat akin to *4 Macc.* 18.6-8). Secondly, the accumulation of examples and quotations from the Scriptures—the catechesis of the seven brothers at the feet of their father—provides a similar catechesis for the author's audience, providing further motivations to heed the exhortation in 18.1-2 to pursue piety through strict Torah-observance.

Finally, 18.1-5 is indispensable to the discourse. Commemorative addresses and diatribes alike could be expected to end with a direct word of exhortation to the audience either to follow the example of the fallen or take to heart and apply the philosophical precept presented. *4 Macc.* 18.1-2 in effect does both. 18.4 must be retained as

Regarding 18 as an interpolation injures the text more than it amends it.

well, since it provides closure by declaring the restoration of the peace and observance of the Law that were breached in 3.20-21. 18.3 and 18.5, that speak of the accomplishment of reward for the martyrs and punishment for the tyrant, are likewise essential for bringing closure to the discourse (and to all the martyrs' declarations of their own vindication throughout the narrative). The text of *4 Maccabees*, therefore, does not require recourse to theories of interpolations or additions.

The esteem which *4 Maccabees* enjoyed in the early church is attested by its appearance in full in two major uncials of the Greek Bible— Alexandrinus (fifth century) and Sinaiticus (fourth century). Vaticanus lacks all four books of the Maccabees, and so the later Codex Venetus (ninth century) becomes an important textual witness. A Syriac version has also survived, which largely follows Sinaiticus against Alexandrinus. The versions that appear in the codices of Josephus's works, being late, are not useful for establishing the text.

Further Reading

Authorship, Date and other General Introductory Issues
The following works may be consulted for further information on introductory matters. In most cases, the views of the authors have been summarized in the discussion above: Amir (1971); Anderson (1985); Bickerman (1976a); Breitenstein (1978); Collins (1983); Deissmann (1900); Dupont-Sommer (1939); Freudenthal (1869); Gilbert (1984); Hadas (1951); Klauck (1989a); Pfeiffer (1949); Townshend (1913); van Henten (1986, 1994). D. S. Williams (1987) has conducted the most thorough examination of the possibility of Josephan authorship of *4 Maccabees*, although he also finally rejects the hypothesis.

Genre
Many of the authors listed above treat the question of the genre of *4 Maccabees*, but especially salient studies have been provided by Norden (1923: 416-20), Lebram (1974) and van Henten (1994). A discussion of genre from the perspective of classical rhetoric appears in deSilva (1995b).

Theon and the Types of Historical Narrative
A concise but helpful discussion of the uses of narrative in classical literature appears in Hadas (1951: 57-59).

Quotations from Seneca, *De constantia*, and Josephus, *Jewish Antiquities*, have been taken from the LCL edition; quotations from Theon, *Progymnasmata*, have been taken from Hadas (1951).

2

4 MACCABEES AND THE JEWISH DIASPORA: SETTING, PURPOSE AND STRATEGY

In the previous chapter I have located *4 Maccabees* rather broadly as an anonymous work by a well-educated, rhetorically skilled Diaspora Jew, writing in an urban environment in the region of Asia or Syria most probably during the first half of the first century CE. Whether the discourse was delivered for a specific festival like Hanukkah or the Feast of Weeks, its meaning and purpose emerges most clearly when we consider it, as does Klauck (1989a: 664), as addressing the 'everyday situation' of Diaspora Judaism. The author and his audience are Hellenistic Jews—Jews who, on the one hand, wished to maintain their ancestral religion and culture but who, on the other hand, had drunk deeply of the Greek values, thought and culture that surrounded them. *4 Maccabees* engages the latter quite fully in order to serve the former, providing us with a unique window into Diaspora Judaism. In this chapter, I will refine my discussion of the author's purpose and strategy by considering the tensions faced by Jews in a Hellenized world, setting forth the contours of the Hellenizing Crisis of 175–164 BCE of which the author reminds his audience, and by investigating how *4 Maccabees* was strategically composed to address these tensions and motivate a response of loyalty to the ancestral ways of Judaism.

Tensions in the Jewish Diaspora

Scholars are generally agreed that there is no necessity to posit a period of anti-Jewish persecution for the writing of *4 Maccabees* (so Townshend 1913: 680; A. O'Hagan 1974: 100-101; van Henten 1995: 317). The issues raised by this discourse would be suitable to a Diaspora Jewish audience at any time during the late Hellenistic and early Roman periods. Throughout this period, however, Jews lived in some tension with their Graeco-Roman environment, a tension which could from time to time erupt into brutal pogroms against the Jewish community (as did in fact occur in Alexandria and Caesarea in the first half of the first century CE; see Philo, *In Flaccum* and Josephus, *Jewish War*, Book 2). The figure of the martyr as the supreme exemplar of the Jewish philosopher thus reflects the extreme end of a continuum of tension within which the audience lived.

Jews living in the Diaspora were torn between the two mutually contradictory principles identified by V. Tcherikover (1961: 346) as 'the ambition to assimilate arising from the Jew's desire to exist among strangers by his individual powers, and the adherence to tradition, induced in the struggle for existence by the need of support from the strong collective organization represented by the community'. Living as a minority culture within the dominant culture of Hellenism, Jews would naturally be drawn to value what the Greeks prized, and to evaluate their own cultural heritage and social location in terms of the standards employed by their Gentile neighbours. They would be caught, in effect, between the values they inherited from their ancestral tradition and the values they learned from their new environment.

The Jews' position was rendered more difficult by a rather persistent strain of anti-Judaism among the representatives of Graeco-Roman culture. The Graeco-Roman authors who addressed the subject of Jews very frequently charged them with anti-social behaviour and with atheism. Hecataeus interpreted Jewish customs and restrictions as misanthropic, and Eratosthenes added that fear of other ethnic groups was typical of barbarians. The rhetorician Apollonius Molon of Rhodes (early first century BCE) wrote that the Jews do not accept people who have other views about God (recorded in Josephus, *Apion* 2.258).

The Greeks and Romans understood piety toward the gods as a reflection of loyalty to the city, as a marker of reliability. The person who knew how to pay proper respect to the gods would know his or her duty in a civic crisis, or would be a reliable partner in business, or would be no fomenter of division in the city. The Jews did not participate in the worship of these gods and were thus never free from suspicion and slander—their devotion to the One God allegedly reflected their concern for the one people, the Jews, and their lack of concern for the public welfare (cf. *3 Macc.* 3.3-7; LXX *Est.* 13.4-5). While usually benefiting from official edicts of toleration, Jews were nevertheless frequently the objects of the dominant culture's hostility on account of these threatening differences, which were usually subsumed under the heading of *misoxenia*, 'hatred of outsiders'. Diodorus of Sicily (34.1-4; 40.3.4), Tacitus (*Histories* 5.5), Juvenal (*Satires*, 14.100-104) and Apion (Josephus *Apion* 2.121) all accuse the Jewish people of supporting their fellow Jews but showing no good will to those who are not of their race. The dietary laws and restrictions on social intercourse practiced by Jews loyal to the Torah, while an effective means of maintaining group boundaries and cohesion, gave rise to anti-Jewish slander from outsiders. Such practices, however commendable from a 'God's-eye view', were regarded by non-Jews in the cities as violations of the ideal of civic unity (cf. *3 Macc.* 3.4, 7). The Jews' loyalty and solidarity was not with the larger *polis*, but rather the *politeuma*, the community within the city, and the Jewish people more broadly. This did not always occur, and we find evidence in Rome, for example, of Jews who were patrons of civic life and fully part of their city; but often, it appears from our sources, they lived as aliens in the city—and that more by their own choice.

These differences became especially evident in the tense and tumultuous circumstances surrounding the attempts of Jews to be granted 'equal citizenship' (*isopoliteia*) with the Greek citizens of Alexandria, Caesarea and other Hellenistic *poleis*. In Alexandria, Antioch and the cities of Ionia the Greek citizens complained that, if the Jews were to be treated as fellow citizens, they should worship the same gods as their Greek neighbours (see Josephus, *Ant.* 12.3.1-2 §§121-26). *3 Maccabees*, while probably legendary, nevertheless reflects the same basic cultural tensions. There, Ptolemy sought to clarify the Jews' civic status by resolving it positively toward integration and full citizenship. This enfranchisement entailed, however, full participation in civic life, where Greek religion embraced all aspects of life—in this case the Dionysiac mysteries (2.27-30; 3.21-23). What Ptolemy saw as the benefaction of the 'priceless citizenship', the Jewish author regarded as 'inflicting public disgrace' because it involved joining fully in the civic life of an idolatrous culture. The message from the outside appears to have been clear: if you Jews desire acceptance within Greek society, and access to all the benefits that accompany it, you must become like us. For the Jews, therefore, the old dilemma remained: remain loyal to the covenant or 'become like the nations'.

Many Jews were willing to make large concessions to the dominant culture in this direction. Some, like Dositheus in *3 Macc.* 1.3 or Philo's nephew, Tiberius Julius Alexander, assimilated themselves completely to the Greek way of life. This was regarded as the path to advancement

4 Maccabees

in social and cultural status, and indeed was actively pursued by many non-Greeks. M. Hengel (1980: 74) correctly notes that 'the initiative towards "Hellenization" was a one-sided one. It came from the indigenous Semitic and Egyptian population, who sought in this way…to share in the prosperity and the success of the Greeks.' The very events that *4 Maccabees* narrates in 3.20-4.26 retain the emphasis on the distinctly Jewish initiative for Hellenization found in both 1 and 2 Maccabees (see 'The Lesson from History', below). 1 Maccabees attributes the initiative to Jews who had accepted fully the dominant culture's criticism of their *ethnos*, and who now regard their separation from the nations as the source of their country's misfortunes (1.11); 2 Maccabees likewise speaks of those Jews 'disdaining the honours prized by their ancestors and putting the highest value upon Greek forms of prestige' (4.15). The relationship between such enthusiastic Hellenizers and loyal Jews was inimical, even brutal: the apostates in Judaea, supported by the military might of Antiochus IV, suppressed loyal observance of the Law by violence; similar hostilities persist in the memory of the author of the Wisdom of Solomon, who speaks of the apostates' antagonism and persecution of the faithful Jew (1.16–2.24). No love was lost in the other direction, as loyal Jews executed apostates after the Hellenizing crisis of 175–164 BCE and fantasized about it in the circles that used *3 Maccabees* (cf. 7.10-15).

How could Jews give up their ancestral religion? E. Bickerman (1976b: 75) suggests that they could reject the Torah specifically because it was the Torah of Moses—it was a human law, like those given by Lycurgus or Zarathustra, not the divine and absolute law. The Law of God was not to be found in any such civil code. Apostates might thus have drawn on the Stoic concept of the Law of Nature as the one true Law and all particular civil or ethnic codes as imperfect, burdensome shadows of it. That such an argument was alive in the Jewish Diaspora, and one which Jews might need to consider and arm themselves against (indeed, one which had made its way into the Jewish community in some way), is shown by its appearance in *4 Macc.* 5.18. Hengel (1974: I, 301) further notes traces of Jewish censure of the Torah as not divine and as containing ludicrous myths (attacked by Philo, *Vit. Mos.* 1.31; *Conf. Ling.* 2).

Jews living in the dominant Hellenistic culture were thus open to criticism from within and without. Their Gentile neighbours often regarded them as unreliable, misanthropic and irreligious; Greek and Latin authors lampooned their dietary laws, circumcision and Sabbath observances (see Chapter 5 below); Jewish apostates attacked the divinity and reliability of the Torah itself and were often themselves a source of hostility. *4 Maccabees* addresses itself to Jews living within such an environment (though not necessarily one of overt hostility), providing a voice that seeks to counterbalance the many negative voices heard by Jews seeking to remain faithful to God's covenant.

The Lesson from History

Part of the author's strategy for addressing the situation of Diaspora Jews involves a return to the events that transpired in Palestine just prior to the accession of Antiochus IV in 175 BCE through the 'Hellenization Crisis', which led to the grisly persecutions and martyrdoms described at length in *4 Maccabees*. The author gravitates to this period not because his audience is once again beset by violent persecution, but because they must face the same question of whether or not to assimilate to the Gentile way of life that precipitated those tumultuous events.

The main sources for the events surrounding this crisis are 1 and 2 Maccabees, Daniel and Josephus's *Antiquities*, book 12. Numerous monographs and articles have been devoted to these sources, their own individual *Tendenzen*, and their reliability for historical reconstruction (the most important of these are given in the 'For Further Reading' section below). It is beyond the scope of this book either to delve into the specific problems of reconstruction or to give adequate attention to the different proposals of the various scholars. Rather, the following pages present what appears to be the most viable reconstruction (tending to favour Hengel 1974 and Bickerman 1976a against Tcherikover 1961 where these disagree, and certainly departing from Goldstein's acceptance [1976: 104-60] of the presentation of Antiochus IV in 1 Maccabees) as the background to *4 Maccabees'* recasting of the story.

The events that form the background to *4 Maccabees* began in 198 BCE when Antiochus III successfully wrested Palestine from Ptolemaic control. He continued the tolerant policy that Judaea had enjoyed under Persian, Greek and Ptolemaic rule, and confirmed the Jewish people's right to self-regulation according to the Torah (cf. Josephus, *Ant.* 12.3.3 §§138-42), an arrangement which continued under Seleucus IV, Antiochus III's son and successor. In an attempt to gain the coastlands of Asia Minor, Antiochus III was defeated by the

Roman armies, which were a rapidly growing power in the
Mediterranean. He died on his return to Syria and was succeeded by
his son, Seleucus IV. Because of heavy financial obligations, Seleucus
attempted through his agent Heliodorus to confiscate the treasures
deposited in the Jerusalem Temple: demonstrations turned Heliodorus
away from his mission, and he eventually murdered his ruler. At this
point, Antiochus IV, another son of Antiochus III (thus the brother of
Seleucus IV), who had been sent to Rome as a hostage after his father's
defeat, was able to seize the throne.

All that occurred in Palestine took place against the background of
the ongoing strife between the Ptolemaic rulers of Egypt and the
Seleucid rulers of Syria, who were fighting to expand their territory
and increase their tribute. Further, the actual crisis in Jerusalem in
169–64 BCE took place also against the background of the struggle for
power over the client people of Judaea between two prominent Jewish
families, namely the house of Tobias and the house of Onias. The
Oniads were a Zadokite high priestly family; the Tobiads, however,
were prominent through the foreign administration of Judaea (Joseph, a
son of Tobias, had been chief tax farmer of Judaea under Ptolemy IV,
before Antiochus III's capture of Palestine). Onias III was high priest at
the time of Antiochus IV's accession. Onias had to leave Jerusalem and
appear in Antioch, the Syrian capital, to answer charges brought against
him by Simon, a supporter of the Tobiad family and the administrator
of the Temple. This strife between the Tobiads and Onias III had its
roots in the restrictions on the market imposed through adherence to
Mosaic law, particularly the prohibitions against any unclean animal
entering the city, a policy which would lower Jerusalem's attractiveness
as a place of commerce to non-Jewish merchants.

After Onias's departure, Jeshua, Onias's more 'progressive' brother,
offered Antiochus IV a large bribe in exchange for his appointment to
the office of high priest. He had his name changed to Jason and came
out clearly in favour of adopting Hellenic customs and institutions in
Judaea. It is very important to note that the motivation and initiative
for Hellenization came from within Judaea. The Seleucids were much
more positive towards the Hellenization of indigenous peoples than
were the Ptolemies. As Hengel (1980: 63) observes, after Rome drove
them out of Asia Minor 'the Seleucids tried to strengthen the
Hellenistic element in their empire by allowing the aristocracy of local
cities to adopt the constitution of a Hellenized *polis* if they so wished,
in return for an appropriate contribution to the royal treasury'. It may

even be said that Antiochus IV 'encouraged' such a policy, but he never forced such a policy upon the subject peoples: this would have compounded the problem he faced on his borders with undue stress within his shrinking empire.

Rather, the initiative towards Hellenization 'came from the indigenous Semitic and Egyptian population, who sought in this way to improve their social and cultural status and to share in the prosperity and the success of the Greeks' (Hengel 1980: 74). The primary sources certainly bear witness to this: 1 Macc. 1.10-11 speaks of renegade Jews who went out to 'make a covenant with the Gentiles around us', who clearly came to believe that their separateness (which led to the Jews' reputation in the ancient world as 'misanthropic' and, essentially, racist) was the cause of their economic and political deprivation. Abandonment of their distinctive traditions was seen by many as the path of socio-economic and political improvement. They sought, like the Tobiad Joseph, to bring 'the Jewish people from poverty and a state of weakness to more splendid opportunities of life' (Josephus, *Ant.* 12.4.10 §224). 2 Maccabees, Daniel and Josephus all likewise attest to the role of apostate Jews (who would rather call themselves 'progressives' or 'reformers') in the Hellenization process. 1 Maccabees and Daniel place an undue stress on Antiochus IV's policies as the source of the Hellenization of Judaea: this reflects rather the propaganda of the local authorities, which was not carefully scrutinized by those 'below' (i.e. the authors of 1 Maccabees and Daniel, who were not in the inside circle of the Hellenizing Jews). The local government led by the Jewish 'reformers' certainly promoted their own policies as the express policy of the king.

Jason, in addition to acquiring the office of high priest, persuaded Antiochus to set aside his predecessors' concessions concerning the Torah, and to refound Jerusalem as a Greek *polis*, 'Antioch at Jerusalem'. Jerusalem must have made considerable progress toward Hellenization before Jason's programme to support the changes that he introduced. Jerusalem was transformed into a Greek city through the establishment of the basic instruments of Greek polity: a gymnasium with a list of young men (ephebes) enrolled to take part; a council; and a list of those enrolled as citizens of the newly created Antioch-at-Jerusalem (a list drawn up by Jason that enabled him to place political power in the hands of the supporters of Hellenization). This policy of voluntary Hellenization had a lot of support among the upper classes (ironically including a large segment of the priestly class). The sources consistently speak of 'many' in Jerusalem enthusiastically taking part in the Greek institutions—even the priests headed for the gymnasium—and many underwent an operation to undo the marks of circumcision, the physical sign of Jewish particularism and separatism. It is also clear that large segments of the population were alienated by these developments, and became the seedbed for dissent, protest and eventually revolution.

These developments received Antiochus's approval, for he visited the city for the first time in 173 BCE and appears not to have changed Jason's programme in any way (2 Macc. 4.21-22). In 172 BCE, the Tobiad family made its move. Menelaus, brother of the Simon who had opposed Onias III and another client of the Tobiads, made a bid to Antiochus IV for the high priesthood, raising Jason's annual tribute by three hundred talents. Antiochus, always looking for more income to finance his planned campaigns against Egypt and other activities, accepted the money and replaced Jason with Menelaus. This was a highly problematic arrangement for the Judaean people: Jason was at least a high priest from the line of Zadok, and therefore had a legitimate claim; Menelaus, of the priestly family of Bilga, had no such claim to the high priesthood. The buying and selling of this office, linked with its subjection to the whim of a foreign ruler, must have been very demoralizing for the people of Judaea. It was of decisive significance for the mysterious group known as the Hasidim, who first appear as pious devotees of the Torah, unwilling even to defend themselves on the Sabbath; they subsequently joined the Maccabaean revolution, but then left the Maccabaean party when Alcimus, a Zadokite, was appointed high priest. It follows that their own opposition activities began when the non-Zadokite Menelaus entered the office of high priest. This change of priesthood appears also to have split the upper class and military personnel: Jason fled from Jerusalem but retained a large number of supporters.

Menelaus is slandered in the sources as a temple-robber, working in collusion with his brother Lysimachus. He managed to alienate the population to such an extent that his brother was killed by a mob, apparently in connection with charges of desecrating the temple through plundering it. Menelaus's own position was becoming rather tenuous, and his rejection by the larger population confirms the hypothesis that the harsh, repressive measures taken against the 'faithful' originate with him.

This relatively static situation (at least from the perspective of Antiochus) became tumultuous after a rumour of Antiochus's death in the middle of his second campaign to take Egypt reached Jerusalem. Jason, who had been waiting his chance, thought that he now had an opportunity to regain control of the high priesthood and hence the effective rule of Judaea. He attacked Menelaus in Jerusalem, driving him back into the citadel. What followed is not spelled out in the sources, whose pro-Hasmonaean slant forbade the recognition of any other armed revolt against the rule of the Hellenizers and their Seleucid overlords. It appears, however, that Jason could not hold control of Jerusalem, being himself driven out by a group hostile to both Jason and Menelaus (possibly the Hasidim, possibly a pro-Ptolemaic faction). This alone accounts for the measures that Antiochus's forces took in Jerusalem, for if Menelaus had regained control after Jason fled, there would have been no need for the massacre that 2 Maccabees recounts.

Antiochus, fearing that Jerusalem was in revolt, left the Egyptian front and retook Jerusalem by force, slaughtering thousands. Antiochus restored Menelaus and fortified his position with more troops, but trouble flared up again so that, in early 167 BCE, Syrian troops under the command of Apollonius again had to enter Jerusalem. Apollonius established the 'Akra', a fortress occupied by Jewish and Syrian soldiers of Antiochus, adjacent to the Temple. Many residents of Jerusalem fled into the countryside; many more were dispossessed of houses and property in order to furnish the settled soldiers. The Temple itself now became the common property of the Jewish and Gentile inhabitants of Antioch-at-Jerusalem, and the worship of the God of Israel was assimilated to the worship of the Syrian 'God of Heaven', Baal Shamin. The sacrifice of swine, the cult prostitutes, the sacred stones all point to Syrian religious practice rather than Greek worship.

The majority of Jews at this point deserted the Temple, which had been polluted by these alien cults. Only the Tobiads, whose only hope for retaining power was Syrian support, heartily endorsed these new developments. It is further believed that Menelaus provided Antiochus with the programme of overturning the Jewish Torah and religion, urging the king to empower him to enforce a decree against Jewish religion in order to provide for the preservation of his power in Judaea. Through destruction of adherence to the conservative, exclusivistic Torah, the extreme Hellenizers hoped to secure their position and advance their programme. That the persecution was locally sponsored is proved by the fact that the Samaritans were allowed to continue their practice in the Temple at Gerizim undisturbed. Menelaus was thus moved with a 'zeal against the Law' comparable to the Hasmonaeans'

'zeal for the Law'. As Bickerman (1976a: 78-79) observes: 'a pagan
king with the simple goal of Hellenizing the Jews would have had no
need to enforce such a prohibition, but it had great importance for a
Jewish reformer anxious to eradicate every particularized custom'.
Menelaus was in a good position to prevail upon the king that such
peculiar religio-political measures were required in Judaea in order to
ensure that no further insurrections would disturb the region.

What followed was a frightful period of religious persecution and an
uncompromising programme of forced apostasy. The stories of brutal-
ity and execution need not be entirely dismissed as aspects of 'pathetic'
history—the episodes of religious intolerance throughout human experience bear witness that there are no limits to human inhumanity.
Certainly the characters and their speeches may be fictitious, but they
may well also have some relationship to historical martyrs.
Circumcision, possession of the Torah, and Sabbath observance were
now all proscribed on pain of death, and officers were sent out to
enforce these rulings throughout Judaea (but *only* within Judaea, again
attesting to the local sponsorship of these actions). Two forms of resistance are preserved by the sources: that of the martyrs who died rather
than abandon their ancestral religion and become colluders with an
unacceptable regime, and that of the revolutionaries led by Mattathias
and his sons.

The author of *4 Maccabees* abbreviates the story found in 2 Maccabees
to highlight the strong statement he wished to make about
Hellenization and the threat this policy carried for the peace of the
Jewish people. First, the narrative demonstrates that assimilation to the
Gentile (Greek) way of life does not lead to social advancement, political opportunity, or economic prosperity but rather to the disturbance
of the peace the Jewish community enjoys when its leaders and members regulate their lives according to the Torah (*4 Macc.* 3.20-21; 18.4).
Peace and stability were the ultimate ideals for an ancient city (cf. Dio
Chrysostom, *Orations* 48.15-16). The ancient world was rather volatile,
and civic unrest was feared for the disruption of everyday life that it
threatened to bring. In an environment where most people lived from
day to day (having no reserves on which to draw in case of emer-
gency), any serious disruption of routine could spell ruin. Intentionally
to disturb the peace and stable order of a city was considered base and
dangerous. The author, therefore, was using the language of political
ethics to further his purpose. The peace of the Jewish *ethnos* depended
on God, their benefactor, which in turn depended on loyalty to the

covenant and striving to live according to the Torah in every respect. Any attempt to advance in the dominant culture at the cost of transgressing the Torah was an act of sedition, of revolution against the common good, since such actions threatened to bring the judgment of God upon the community. Such attempts should rouse the censure of the community rather than its admiration and emulation.

Secondly, the author's presentation of this story in 3.18-4.26 reinforces for the audience the reality and efficacy of the Deuteronomistic covenant. As long as the nation chooses to remain loyal to the Torah, God protects his faithful clients; when Jews begin to think that breaking the covenant would lead to advantage, and choose to violate the Torah, then divine chastisement falls upon the nation (see Chapter 6 below). In the world of the narrative, Antiochus regards the ingestion of defiling food (4.26) as the symbol of renouncing Judaism. The author was concerned that Jews understand that it was not a smaller thing to transgress the dietary regulations of the Torah than to commit apostasy or murder—any despite shown the Law was a dangerous affront to God. There were to be no points of negotiation with the dominant culture as far as keeping the Torah was concerned: the regulations that maintained Jewish distinctiveness, such as circumcision, dietary laws, and Sabbath observances were not to be compromised for the sake of any hoped-for peace with the Graecized world. The historical precedent of Jason was set forward in order to dispel any optimistic appraisal of such a plan. The narration of the crisis of 167–164 BCE was shaped to move its Jewish audience to take the whole Law seriously, since each commandment was invested with the integrity of the whole Torah: each act of obedience contributed to the peace of the nation; each violation for the sake of joining with the Gentile nations threatened to bring down God's wrath upon them.

The Purpose of *4 Maccabees*

Many of the tensions and criticisms noted in the first section of this chapter are reflected in *4 Maccabees* itself, particularly in the speeches placed on the lips of Antiochus IV. The hypothesis that *4 Maccabees* seeks to strengthen Jews for a coming persecution (Townshend 1913: 654) presumes too narrow a range of applicability: the temptation to depart from the Torah was ever present, as the advantages of doing so were ever present. Duress and persecution were not required for a crisis of commitment to seize the individual Jew, or even a large segment of a community. B. Heininger (1989: 55) correctly observes that the philosophical question posed by *4 Macc.* 1.1 has a very concrete context, namely the balance between assimilation and retreat into a ghetto, between abandonment of a distinct identity and commitment to a tradition that is threatened with dissolution. The author of *4 Maccabees* does not seek assent to a philosophical proposition, but rather seeks commitment to the way of life exemplified by the martyrs (cf. van Henten 1994: 69; 1995: 317), the way of life which, the author claims, fulfils the highest ideals of Hellenistic ethical philosophy. Thus the Greek-sounding invitation to 'pay earnest attention to philosophy' in 1.2 becomes the very Jewish exhortation to 'obey this law and exercise piety in every way' (18.1). The author's demonstration seeks to show that the sort of reason that achieves the Greek ideal of virtue is devout reason, which is reason choosing wisdom as taught in God's law, the Jewish Torah. Redditt (1983: 249) rightly perceives that the rule of reason over the passions is 'only the formal and not the crucial focus'—obedience to the Torah is the primary concern, for which the philosophical thesis becomes a sort of cipher.

The author of *4 Maccabees* seeks to demonstrate to Jews that their own cultural and religious heritage already shows the surest way to attain the ideal of virtue that the Greeks claim to prize as honourable, yet fail to achieve because they are alienated from the One God. He continues the martyrs' struggle to preserve the 'way of life of the Hebrews', and enlists the audience in this struggle as well. He does not do this, however, by retreating from dialogue with the dominant culture. Both he and his audience are not isolated from the Hellenistic culture: in the author there is clear evidence of the penetration of this dominant culture. His language (the fluent use of Greek), intellect (the familiarity with a broad range of Greek ethical thought), rhetoric (completely analysable in terms of classical Greek rhetoric, literary forms, and categories of argumentation), and values (accepting and using the cardinal virtues of the Stoics and Platonists) show quite an advanced degree of 'Hellenization'. The author does, however, draw the line rather clearly: Pharaoh's gold is valuable, but his religion is not. He listens carefully to the voices of the Greek ethical philosophers, borrowing many ideas from the Platonists, Peripatetics and Stoics in order to make Judaism more intelligible to its own adherents, who have themselves internalized many of the values of those 'outside' voices. He gives the heritage of his audience respectability in terms of the values and standards of the ethical pioneers of the Hellenistic world, so that

the audience will not abandon its way of life as valueless but rather recognize its greater value. The author sympathizes with the audience's
desire for advancement, but he turns its ambitions back toward the
eternal advantages that attend loyalty to God (13.14-17), praising those
martyrs who recognized the meagre value of temporary advantages
purchased at the cost of exchanging God's favour for divine wrath.

The author chooses the martyrs of the Hellenizing crisis as the best
and noblest exemplars of virtue (specifically, of reason's mastery of the
passions), not because the audience faces similar loss, but rather because
the extreme case facilitates the moderate case. The audience may better
tolerate the economic or social privation it will experience having witnessed both the endurance of the martyrs and the praiseworthy remembrance and eternal honour that followed their courage and loyalty. The
martyrs' choices and responses represent the honourable ones. Some
hearers or readers of the work may themselves have been ready to
capitulate to the demand of their Gentile neighbours to 'become like
them', leaving behind the more obvious markers of Jewish exclusivism
(such as dietary and purity regulations that limit social intercourse
between Jews and non-Jews, Sabbath observances, perhaps even the
strict avoidance of idolatry). Some may have come under the influence
of the 'Stoic' critique of the Jewish law (as an imperfect, partial, burdensome code).

For the different needs of the individuals who made up such communities, *4 Maccabees* promises to achieve different effects. For those
Jews committed to the Torah, the author presents material to reinforce
that commitment and to strengthen them for the endurance of whatever disadvantages would accompany identification with the Jewish
race and the complete avoidance of idolatry and the like; for wavering
or confused Jews, the author presents material to exhort them to take a
stand for the Torah and piety, calling them back to commitment to
Jewish particularism as the means of achieving the highest honour and
reputation; for Jews feeling the threat of Hellenism especially deeply, or
experiencing deprivation on account of their loyalty to ancestral ways,
the author provides examples to promote endurance and courage to
face the contest. Claims such as that found in 2.23 ('one who lives subject to [the law] will rule a kingdom that is temperate, just, good and
courageous') and many like it would have been heard in different ways
by different hearers: the author's choice of epideictic oratory as the
means to achieve his end allowed for this ambiguity, such that the same
piece may have encouraged the committed and challenged the waver-

ing. The purpose, however, remains constant: to encourage Jews in an environment where assimilation into the dominant culture may seem advantageous to pursue the greater advantage of remaining faithful to God and the Torah.

While he does not seek it himself (explicitly addressing his discourse to Jews, 18.1), the author brings Jewish self-expression to a point where closer conversation with the Greek world becomes possible and potentially fruitful. The author identifies the need for Jews to educate the inhabitants of the Graeco-Roman world in the matters of true honour and piety by remaining firm in witness to God and devotion to God's educative Law. Antiochus embodies the extremes of their errors. Gentiles need to learn true respect for God as creator and benefactor (12.11)—that is, instruction in piety; they need to learn true respect for other human beings as God's clients (12.13, cf. 3.15-16); they need to learn about the honourable and the just from the true perspective of God's standards of virtue and the praiseworthy (11.6). Later missionaries could certainly use his material in their efforts to extend the covenant of Abraham to the other nations that were to be included in the blessing, promoting now to outsiders the value of the Torah as a philosophical discipline and a means to achieve virtue and mastery of the passions. Like the martyrs, the audience, too, is involved in a noble contest (16.16), striving for virtue and fidelity to God, striving with the other cultures of the world to bear witness to them, thus relating with them salvifically. They may learn from them, as has the author (for example, in his use of Greek ideals and modes of argument), but may not be beaten by them through assimilation.

Rhetorical Strategy of *4 Maccabees*

Discussion of the text itself may usefully be preceded by comments on its rhetorical strategy—its means of persuasion. In Chapter 1, I looked at the genre or form of *4 Maccabees*, and concluded that it combined elements of the diatribe (a philosophical demonstration) and the commemorative address (an encomium) into what now functioned as a protreptic discourse (a work that promotes a certain way of life). In all of these aspects, *4 Maccabees* functions primarily as what ancient rhetoricians would have called epideictic rhetoric. While deliberative rhetoric is concerned with explicitly urging a particular course of action (usually one over against another) in a council chamber, and forensic rhetoric deals with assigning guilt or establishing innocence in a legal proceeding, epideictic rhetoric sought to define or affirm essential cultural values. Thus, the funeral oration would often praise the dead on the basis of the virtues they had embodied.

The epideictic speech, however, also sought some response from the audience, which was generally that they should also make it their aim to devote themselves to a particular virtue or to defend the city's way of life. The close of Pericles' Funeral Oration (Thucydides, *Histories* 2.35-45) commends the courageous, fallen soldiers as examples to the living, calling them so to value the Athenian way of life as to die to preserve it. As G. Kennedy (1984: 74) has noted, funeral orations and the like 'take on a more or less subtle deliberative purpose', though in a much more general way than a true deliberative speech. Praise of others was only acceptable insofar as the hearers believed themselves capable of the same achievements (so in Thucydides, *Histories* 2.35.2). The philosophical demonstration is also a species of epideictic rhetoric: while in the purest sense it sought only assent to an argument, in the form of diatribe that becomes the vehicle of ethical philosophy it also asks the hearers to consider the value of a particular way of life, and often seeks a commitment from the audience to follow it.

It is in this sense that *4 Maccabees* offers an example of epideictic rhetoric. It, too, seeks to strengthen the audience's commitment to particular cultural values, namely the strict observance of the Torah, as its general policy of action. The author proposes the demonstration of a philosophical thesis ('devout reason is sovereign over the emotions', 1.1), but indicates from the introduction that this will include the praise of 'those who died for the sake of virtue' (1.8), namely the Jewish martyrs, as the supreme proof of the thesis. What the author goes on to do, however, is to demonstrate that the path of virtue (hence to honour) is actually the path of Torah-observance, even in those particulars that cause so much tension between Jews and non-Jews (i.e. the dietary regulations, 1.30-35). It is by strict observance of the Jewish law that the Stoic and Peripatetic ideals of the sage as king (2.21-23) and as free person (5.38) become reality. The martyrs themselves are praised for their dedication to piety, for their courageous endurance, and for their superiority to all external compulsions. They are held up as examples to encourage the pursuit of virtue (through uncompromising obedience to the Torah) in the same way that the fallen Athenian soldiers are put forward as the best of men by Pericles. It is expected that the author's praise of their achievement will rouse emulation in the hearts of the hearers, reaffirming for them that the path of the Torah (rather

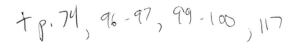

+ p. 74, 96-97, 99-100, 117

than the path of compromise) may indeed be the surest path to fulfil their highest ambitions.

The protreptic aim of the whole work is advanced by the author's creation of a deliberative environment within the larger epideictic framework. Within the narrative demonstration, there appear two opposing 'counsellors' in the martyrs' arena, who are juxtaposed in 9.2-3: 'Moses our counsellor' and the 'counsellor of lawlessness', namely Antiochus. Antiochus is given short deliberative speeches, which reflect the Graeco-Roman culture's unsympathetic understanding of Jewish culture and present strong cases for the rejection of the Torah in favour of joining the dominant culture (5.5-13; 8.5-14). In these speeches he seeks to 'advise' (5.6; 8.5) the Jews, much as the audience's Gentile neighbours and more liberal co-religionists may have done. These enticements are met, however, with even stronger rejoinders from Eleazar and the seven brothers (5.16-38; 9.1-9). These speeches provide the rationale for the faithful Jew's refusal to compromise obedience to the Torah. As such, they directly serve the protreptic aim of the discourse, no longer simply demonstrating to the audience that 'devout reason is master of the emotions', but that the Torah must zealously be kept by God's client people if they are to receive approval as noble and virtuous in the eternal court of reputation.

Setting these deliberations within the epideictic frame allows the author to evaluate each course of action in terms of honour and dishonour, nobility and baseness. *Ethos*, the perceived reliability and nobility of the speaker, was an essential element of persuasion. This author is able to undermine the arguments for accommodation by presenting Antiochus as a completely unreliable, shameless and vicious character. The arguments themselves are tainted by being connected with this tyrant. The author is further able to characterize the path of accommodation as 'cowardly and unmanly' (8.16), but to praise the course that the martyrs approved as the essence of virtue and the path to the greater honour and advantage (since it leads to eternal honour in the presence of the Divine Patron).

The audience is thus made to identify with the martyrs, but also to desire to emulate their choices so that they, too, will be approved as courageous, just and pious. *4 Maccabees* holds up a pattern of how to act honourably, and thus how to assure an honourable remembrance. Just as the martyrs are considered 'blessed for the honour in which they are held' (1.10), so also those who embody their values will enjoy esteem both during life (within the minority culture) and after death (before

God and the company of the ancestors). The martyrs' exhortations to
one another (e.g. 6.22; 9.23-24; 13.9-18) become, thus, exhortations
to the audience. The mother's words to her sons become her words to
the Diaspora Jewish community: 'noble is the contest to which you are
called to bear witness for the nation. Fight zealously for our ancestral
law... Remember that it is through God that you have had a share in
the world and have enjoyed life, and therefore you ought to endure
any suffering for the sake of God' (16.16-19). These listeners would no
doubt have had to consider the applicability of such advice to their
own situations. The 'hortatory' potential of epideictic rhetoric is thus
intensified. By the time the audience receives the final exhortation,
they have ample cause to find honour and advantage both in their
Jewish identity ('O Israelite children, offspring of the seed of Abraham')
and in the policy that the demonstration recommends as the basis for all
their dealings ('obey this law and exercise piety in every way', 18.1).

Further Reading

The Encounter between Judaism and Hellenism
A general introduction to the issue of Hellenization and Jewish responses to it
can be found in Russell (1972: 13-40). Collins (1983) and Newsome (1992)
provide a closer investigation of the influence of Hellenism on the Jewish literature of the Hellenistic and Roman periods, the latter also serving as a general
introduction to the beliefs and culture of Judaism during this time. The classic
study of the Hellenization of Palestine was provided by Hengel (1974), who
also offers a second book (Hengel 1980) exploring the nature of the
Hellenization programme of Alexander and his successors and the ways in
which Hellenization affected Jewish life in Palestine and the Diaspora. DeSilva
(1996b) examines Ben Sira's attempt to sustain commitment to the Jewish way
of life against the encroachments of Hellenization in the generation before the
outbreak of the 'Hellenization crisis'.

Jews and Anti-Judaism in the Graeco-Roman World
Gager (1983) provides a rich discussion of primary sources on pro- and anti-
Judaism in the Hellenistic and Roman periods. Smallwood (1981) has written
the classic study on the effects of Roman rule on Jewish life, largely in Palestine
and Alexandria. Especially useful are her discussions of the anti-Jewish riots in
Alexandria of 38–41 CE.

The 'Hellenization Crisis' and Maccabaean Revolt
Reconstruction of the precise history of the 'Hellenization crisis' prior to the
outbreak of the Maccabaean Revolt is complicated by the conflicting data in

the primary sources. Harrington (1988) has ably analysed the *tendenz* of each of
these sources (1 and 2 Maccabees; Daniel; Josephus) and attempted a historical
reconstruction based on the data that are not shaped by the interests of these
authors. He builds on the work of four scholars in particular whose contributions are essential to an appreciation of the complexity of the dynamics of the
period and the difficulties of the historian's task. Bickerman (1976b) proposes
that the initiative for Hellenization came from the Jerusalem aristocracy and
that the source of the persecution of 167–164 BCE was initiated and directed by
Menelaus, the Hellenizing high priest. Tcherikover (1961) and Bickerman
agree that Hellenization was locally initiated, but Tcherikover sees the persecution as Antiochus's response to a revolt that broke out in Jerusalem prior to the
rise of the Maccabees. He surmises that the particular shape of the 'abomination
of desolation' involved the introduction of Syrian cults into the Jerusalem
Temple, to accommodate the soldiers garrisoned in that city. Goldstein (1976;
1983) reads the Hellenization crisis largely as the result of Antiochus IV's initiative for the cultural and political unification of his empire, a view which most
scholars have rejected, while Hengel (1974) supports Bickerman's interpretation of the repression of the Torah as the result of 'zeal against the Torah'
among apostate, Hellenized Jews.

Argumentation in the Graeco-Roman World
Primary sources for investigation of rhetorical theory in the Graeco-Roman
world include Aristotle, *The Art of Rhetoric*, Quintilian, *Institutes (Institutio
Oratoria)*, and Pseudo-Cicero, *Rhetorica ad Herennium*. General introductions to
the subject, together with models for application of classical rhetorical theory to
the analysis of New Testament texts, can be found in Mack (1990) and
Kennedy (1984). Although primarily oriented toward the Synoptic Gospels,
the introductory chapters of Mack and Robbins (1989: 1-67) provide an accessible discussion of some basic elements of classical argumentation, particularly
relating to the elaboration of a *chreia*. Classical sources on the elements of the
elaboration, which are also basic building blocks of argumentation in the
ancient world, have been collected in Hock and O'Neil (1986). DeSilva
(1995a: 37-144) discusses the ways in which honour and dishonour are used in
classical and Hellenistic argumentation, with a special emphasis on how such
rhetoric contributes to the maintenance of a particular culture in a multicultural
environment. The importance of honour discourse for understanding how
4 Maccabees would have been heard by its audience is the topic of deSilva
(1995b). Klauck (1989b) provides a detailed rhetorical analysis of *4 Macc.* 1.1-
12 as a classical *exordium*, or introduction to an oration.

Quotations from Josephus, *Against Apion* and *Jewish Antiquities*, have been taken
from the LCL editions of these works.

3

4 MACCABEES AS PHILOSOPHICAL DEMONSTRATION

The author leads the audience to hear his work as philosophical discourse by presenting his topic as 'most philosophical' from the outset. He promises a philosophical demonstration that devout reason—that is, close observance of the Jewish Torah—is able to control the passions that hinder virtue. Indeed, this statement holds the whole work together, reappearing throughout like a refrain (1.1, 7, 13, 30; 2.6, 7, 9; 6.31-35; 13.1-5; 16.1; 18.2). This proposition (in the shorter form, 'reason masters the passions') surfaces frequently in Hellenistic ethical philosophy, and was close to the heart of philosophy itself according to several authors (Plutarch, 'On Moral Virtue', 1 [*Moralia* 440D]; *Letter of Aristeas to* [*Philocrates*] 221-22), reaching back to Platonic ethics (*Phaedo* 93-94; *Phaedrus*). Our author uses the ethical weight of this proposition, and the desirability of the virtue that it promises, to maintain commitment to the ancestral traditions of Diaspora Judaism. We have already seen that this is not a dry, academic exercise, but rather a discourse that energetically promotes a way of life, much like Epictetus's *Discourses* or Seneca's 'On the Firmness of the Wise Person' (*De constantia*).

Various scholars have emphasized a special closeness between *4 Maccabees* and either Stoic (Deissmann 1900: 151; Renehan 1972), Peripatetic (Dupont-Sommer 1939: 54) or Platonic (Hadas 1953: 101, 116-17) ethical philosophy, but all would basically agree that this author cannot be assigned to any particular philosophical school. Rather, he draws his material from the so-called 'philosophical *koinē*', the popular moral philosophy proclaimed by sophists in the streets or shared by all educated people as part of the common cultural heritage of the Hellenized Mediterranean. There is no justification, however, for calling this author a 'dilettante' (so Schürer 1986: 590) who gave his Judaism a mere 'philosophical veneer'. Rather, he strategically combined elements from a number of philosophical schools (granted, not necessarily knowing the original sources of each idea) to form an ethical philosophy useful for promoting rigorous adherence to the Jewish Torah.

The first verses capture the attention and good will of the hearers, promising to speak of a 'most philosophical' topic that is full of the promise of 'knowledge' about things essential to attaining virtue for attentive hearers. Virtue was a desirable goal for any audience (except the most shameless) in the Graeco-Roman world, since virtue was considered the criterion for honour. Rather than speak of the Stoic or Cynic way of life, this 'most philosophical' speech celebrates the benefits of following the Torah. Many Diaspora Jews presented the Jewish way of life as a philosophy (a term broad enough to include 'way of life'). In his *Jewish War*, Josephus speaks of the different 'parties' within Judaism as differing schools of philosophy whose disagreements mirror those which existed between Greek philosophical schools. Philo commonly refers to Judaism as a 'philosophy' (cf. *Leg. Gai.* 156, 245) and the author of the *Letter of Aristeas to Philocrates* (31) speaks of the legislation of the Torah as 'most philosophical' and worthy of a place in the library of Alexandria. While 'philosophy' covers a broad range of areas of inquiry (physics, psychology, politics, metaphysics, etc.), in authors most concerned with ethics, or 'living nobly', philosophy 'consists in the collection of rational arguments' that supply 'aid and support for leading a good and happy life' (Cicero, *Tusculun Disputations* 4.84). As it is defined in the *Letter of Aristeas* (256), philosophy is rather centrally concerned with the very topic we find in *4 Maccabees*:

> It is to deliberate well over every contingency and not to be carried away by impulses, but to ponder the injuries which are the outcome of the passions, and to perform the duties of the moment properly, with passions moderated.

Presenting Judaism as a 'philosophy' is meant to make it both intelligible and respectable, if not in the eyes of outsiders at least in the eyes of Jews who are thoroughly imbued with Hellenistic culture. The author of *4 Maccabees* thus takes his place beside Philo, the author of the *Letter of Aristeas*, and Aristobulus in the task of preserving the meaningfulness of following Judaism in a thoroughly Hellenistic world.

The Philosophical Thesis

The author begins his oration with a statement of the thesis that 'devout reason is sovereign over the emotions (*pathē*)' (1.1). The Greek term *pathē* is a rather complex idea: in English one would use 'emotions', 'desires' and 'sensory experiences' to cover a comparable semantic range (I will simply use 'emotions' or 'passions' for convenience in this discussion). In popular ethical philosophy, the passions are the enemy of virtue: people are kept from living virtuously because of the power of the passions and the powerlessness of the undisciplined reasoning faculty to control them (see the *Letter of Aristeas* 277). Plutarch (*On Moral Virtue* 1 [*Moralia* 440D]) writes that ethical virtue 'has as its material the emotions of the soul and as its form reason', such that the former are subject to the latter. Some measure of 'training' (*askēsis*) is required for the reason to attain the upper hand, as, for example, Galen and Epictetus acknowledge. The importance of the author's subject ('essential', 1.2) should be recognized by his hearers simply on the basis of their knowledge of popular philosophy. His speech will assist their 'reason' to master the 'passions', and so advance their ability to live virtuously, and thus to acquire honour (in their own eyes, if not in the eyes of their Gentile neighbours).

Most Stoic authors advocated the extirpation of passions, hence *apatheia* was their goal. They regarded passions as evils and found even a 'moderate' use of an evil thing to be unacceptable for the wise person (Cicero, *Tusculun Disputations* 3.22; 4.38, 57). *4 Maccabees* agreed with Plato (cf. *Phaedo* 93-94), Posidonius and the Peripatetics that the passions were to be controlled, or moderated (*metriopathein*), and not destroyed (cf. Plutarch, *On Moral Virtue* 3 [*Moralia* 442A-443D]). The author of the *Letter of Aristeas* (221-22), not surprisingly, expressed the same conviction as *4 Maccabees*: in response to the question, 'What is the highest rule?', the answer is given, 'To rule oneself and not be carried away by passions... Yet in all things moderation is a good principle. What God gives take and hold; do not long for what is out of reach.'

Plutarch argued that extirpating the passions would be 'neither possible nor expedient'. The authors of the *Letter of Aristeas* and of *4 Maccabees* share this view, although perhaps for different reasons. For these Jewish authors, the belief that the passions were part of the divinely created order lay behind their reluctance to dispense with them entirely. In the *Letter of Aristeas*, the passions allow one to enjoy the good things that God gives, which one is to accept with gratitude: reason prevents the passions from becoming instruments of evil, and the individual from reaching for more than is divinely given or permitted. For the author of *4 Maccabees*, God is the one who has implanted 'emotions and inclinations' in the human being in creation (2.21-23): to uproot what God has planted is beyond human ability. God's created hierarchy, however, must be preserved: reason, subject to the Law, must govern the senses (through which the passions enter). The author will return to defend this particular nuance of the thesis in 3.2-18.

The distinctive note of *4 Maccabees'* statement of the thesis is, of course, the addition of the adjective 'devout' or 'pious' (*eusebēs*) to the faculty of 'reason' (*logismos*). S. Lauer (1955: 170) understands this as an oxymoron or paradox; others view it more as a tautology, since for the Stoic all reasoning is grounded in the divine *logos*. It is in fact neither an oxymoron nor a tautology. The author chooses *logismos*, 'reasoning' (already used by Stoics in direct opposition to *thumos*, 'passion'), rather than the more philosophically loaded term *logos* ('the divine mind'). The epithet 'devout' qualifies the sort of 'reasoning' that masters the passions and makes possible a virtuous, noble, praiseworthy life. While the point is not developed here, the use of this adjective allowed the author over the course of the discourse to link 'Torah-observance' and 'living virtuously' closely together.

The author does not provide a technical discussion of how the passions hinder virtue: he takes it for granted that his readers will concur on this point. What he does wish to prove is *devout* reason's mastery of these hindrances to virtue; that is, he will seek to establish that piety (to be linked with Torah-observance) is itself the path to virtue, and to the self-respect and honour that the Diaspora Jew craves. This form of 'reasoning' masters the passions that hinder self control, justice and courage (1.3-4). At this point we should note a tension: the dominant culture tended to regard the pious Jews with contempt for holding to xenophobic laws and customs and for honouring only their own God. The author was aware of this tension, and so built into his discourse several ancillary considerations. First, not all Gentiles have knowledge of virtue, and so do not behave fittingly toward the virtuous. Antiochus himself provided the example of this type (11.4-6; 12.11-14). Secondly, the higher arena for honour is not the Graeco-Roman society (as the apostate Jews supposed) but the court of God, whose verdicts are eternal (13.14-17; 16.24-25). The author holds out the possibility that Gentiles may eventually recognize the virtue and honour of the Torah-observant Jew (17.17, 23), but he does not direct his audience's hopes to this eventuality. The loyalty of the Jew will not depend on the Gentile's approval.

Having clearly stated his thesis and gained the attention and good will of the audience, the author turns in the second half of the *exordium* to the manner of demonstration. The primary proof for the thesis (after a discussion of how specific laws from the Torah enable one to master specific passions) will come from an examination of the examples of Eleazar and the seven brothers and their mother who endured being tortured to death for the sake of virtue (1.7-9) rather than willingly to transgress the Torah (5.28-34). Examples are recognized as an inductive form of proof in classical rhetoric, and the author's choice of those who accepted death rather than assimilation into the Greek way of life as examples is surely significant for the impact his work will have on his audience. Within the *exordium* (the introduction) of his speech, the author has already made two important steps toward achieving his purpose. First, he has captured the hearers' interest in his speech because it promises to lead them to virtue and honour, and he has prepared for his demonstration that the Torah enables reason to govern the passions. Secondly, he has established through his choice of examples that attaining the highest degree of virtue—even as this is defined by Greek ethicists—is not incompatible with holding fast to the Jewish Law. The choice of those who faced the extreme loss as exemplars of *kalokagathia*, the highest Greek ideal of virtue, was no doubt intended to help Diaspora Jews facing the whole range of loss (from moderate disadvantage to outright persecution on account of their customs) to conquer the passions that weakened their resolve and to maintain their commitments in the face of hostility, to 'endure for the sake of virtue'.

Definitions of Terms: *4 Maccabees* 1.13–30a

The author appropriately begins his proof by providing a definition of 'reason' (1.15-19) and by exploring the character of 'passion' as that which leads to vice (1.20-29). After these preliminary matters, he shows at some length in 1.30b–3.18 how reason is able to master each kind of passion that he lists in 1.20-29.

The author's definition of 'reason' incorporates much material that is common to Greek philosophical discourse:

> Now reason is the mind that with sound logic prefers the life of wisdom. Wisdom, next, is the knowledge of divine and human matters and the causes of these. This, in turn, is education in the law, by which we learn divine matters reverently and human affairs to our advantage. Now the kinds of wisdom are rational judgment, justice, courage, and self-control. Rational judgment is supreme over all of these, since by means of it reason rules over the emotions (1.15-19).

4 Maccabees does not involve itself in the discussions concerning the parts of the soul, and in what parts dwells the rational and irrational faculties. Reason for him is really an activity rather than a part of the soul—it becomes manifest when the mind prefers 'with sound logic' the 'life of wisdom'. 'Sound logic' is here a technical expression found in Greek ethicists for the mental processes leading to the choice of virtue over vice (Plato, *Phaedo* 93E): possessing this sort of 'sound logic' is itself the whole goal of philosophy (Epictetus, *Discourses* 4.8.12). The formal definition of 'wisdom' that follows in 1.16 comes word-for-word from the Hellenistic philosophers (Cicero, *Tusculun Disputations* 4.26.57; Seneca *Epistulae Morales* 89.5; Philo, *Congr.* 79). Renehan (1972: 228) points out that this definition is not the peculiar province of Stoics, but enjoyed a wider currency.

The author departs from these philosophers, however, in 1.17, where his own distinctive interests and philosophical allegiances come to the fore. While 'Greeks desire wisdom' (1 Cor. 1.22), Jews also had pursued wisdom extensively, and *4 Maccabees* is clearly rooted in Jewish wisdom traditions in his definition. Proverbs had long ago identified 'wisdom' with 'the fear of the Lord', an identification that was intensified in the Septuagint, which frequently adds the phrase 'and to know the Law is good understanding' (LXX Prov. 9.10; 13.15; *my translation*). Ben Sira, living during the period when the inhabitants of Judaea were increasingly influenced by Hellenism and seeking to combat this trend, wrote: 'if you desire wisdom, keep the commandments' (1.26); 'in all wisdom there is the fulfilment of the law' (19.20). Following in this tradition, *4 Maccabees* defines wisdom as 'education in the Law': the twofold curriculum of 'wisdom', namely divine and human matters, is fully covered by the Torah's instruction. Obeying the commandments leads both to advantageous human relationships and to the maintenance of proper reverence for God. The importance of this second aspect of wisdom was known to both Jews and Greeks, whose tragedies portray the fearful consequences of arrogating to human privilege what belongs to the gods alone (cf. Sophocles, *Antigone* 1347-52). *4 Maccabees* is in many respect like *Antigone*: the martyrs, like Antigone, suffer on account of piety and justice and are considered honourable; Antiochus IV, like Creon, comes to grief and censure on account of his lack of piety toward God.

Just as the author will show the different kinds of passion, so he first sets forward the different species of 'wisdom', under the heads of the four cardinal virtues: prudence (rational judgment), justice, courage, and self control (1.18). While the list of traits recognized as virtuous in the ancient world could be extended, these four are frequently cited in both Greek and Jewish authors as a sort of shorthand for the full range (cf. Wis. 8.7; Cicero, *Rhetorica ad Herennium* 3.2.3). Noteworthy is this author's elevation of prudence, or 'rational judgment', to a position of pre-eminence among the four. This follows the thinking of Zeno of Citium, who, according to Plutarch (*On Moral Virtue* 2 [*Moralia* 441A]),

> defines prudence as justice when it is concerned with what must be rendered to others as their due, as temperance when concerned with what must be chosen or avoided, as fortitude when concerned with what must be endured.

The rise of prudence to the head of the four arises from the identification of the passions as the 'fountainhead of all disorders' (Cicero, *Tusculun Disputations* 4.22). The focus on the contest between right reason and the passions raises the importance of prudence, the virtue that enables the choosing of virtue over vice.

Reason, then, is defined at first in terms congenial to the wider Graeco-Roman philosophical discussion: as this formal definition proceeds, however, the more functional definition that emerges equates wisdom (the tutor of reason) with the instructions of the Torah. There is no chance here of reading *nomos* as something other than the Jewish Law, for, as the demonstration proceeds in 1.30b–2.23, it is precisely the dictates of the Torah that are in view, and, as the martyr narratives indicate, it is Moses whose counsel the heroes receive (9.2), and the Torah which stands as the instructor in virtue that they refuse to abandon (5.22-24).

The author provides no actual definition of the passions, such as one finds in Zeno: 'a violent movement or assault of (upon) the soul, which is irrational and contrary to nature' (Diogenes Laertius, *Lives* 7.110). He does, however, construct a rather elegant taxonomy of them. Here he does not give the fourfold definition of the Stoics (distress, fear, desire, pleasure; Cicero, *Tusculun Disputations* 4.9-22; Diogenes Laertius, *Lives* 7.110). Rather, he follows Aristotle's more basic division of the passions into two types: pain and pleasure, which take on different forms in various contexts (*Rhetoric* 2.1). These two basic passions (here clearly in the sense of 'experiences') operate on both body and soul (1.20) and have both precursors and consequences: 'desire precedes pleasure and delight follows it. Fear precedes pain and sorrow comes after' (1.23). His definition of anger as an 'emotion embracing pleasure and pain' is directly derived from Aristotle as well, according to whom anger is 'a longing, accompanied by pain, for...revenge for a real or apparent slight, affecting a man himself or one of his friends', together with 'a certain pleasure, due to the hope of revenge to come' (*Rhetoric* 2.2.1-2). He concludes his taxonomy of the types of passion with a warning concerning the 'malevolent tendency' that even exists in pleasure. This suggests that the authors of *4 Maccabees* and the *Letter of Aristeas* share the conviction that some pleasures, being given by God, are indeed good, but that even pleasure, which God implanted as a blessing, can be perverted into something evil. In both the soul and the body, this is manifested as a perversion of the good gift of God, or as an overreaching beyond what is licit and just.

Passion, then, though undefined, is shown to refer to desires, emotions and sensate experiences. Through any of these, a person is in danger of being turned from the virtuous course of action. For example, through the emotion of fear or the physical experience of pain a person may fail to exhibit courage and fall short of virtue; in the grip of anger or desire, a person may be led to usurp God's privileges (e.g. by taking vengeance) or claim pleasures that God has not permitted (e.g. fornication or adultery). The role of reason with regard to the 'many offshoots' of the two main plants of passions (pleasure and pain, 1.28) is likened to that of the gardener: 'the master cultivator, reason, weeds and prunes and ties up and waters and thoroughly irrigates, and so tames the jungle of habits and emotions' (1.29). Notably, the role of reason, the gardener, is not to uproot (as in Cicero, *Tusculun Disputations* 4.57), but to cultivate healthy passions and prune away every excess that threatens virtue. This is a figure used frequently by Philo:

> like a good farmer, the virtuous man eradicates in the wild wood all the mischievous young saplings which have been planted by the passions or by the vices, but leaves untouched all those that bear fruit, and which may act as a wall and prove a firm defence for the soul. And, again, among the trees capable of cultivation he manages them in different ways, and not all in the same way: pruning some and adding props to others, training some so as to increase their size, and cutting down others so as to keep them dwarf (*Det. Pot. Ins.* 105; cf. also *Leg. All.* 1.47).

This diversity of cultivating techniques is, in effect, the subject of 1.30b–2.23, in which the different commands of the Torah are shown to effect the pruning of excess and cultivation of virtue according to the different requirements of each passion.

The Examples of Devout Reason's Mastery over the Passions

Unlike Philo, the author of *4 Maccabees* uses no examples outside the sacred history of Israel and uses no text to support his argument save for the Jewish Scriptures. This is in keeping with his conviction that 'the children of the Hebrews alone are invincible where virtue is concerned' (9.18) and therefore provide the surest examples of virtue, together with his conviction that the Torah is God's sufficient provision for the human's quest for virtue. He proceeds loosely to group these references to the Torah and examples from Israel's past under the headings of self-control (1.30b–2.6a) and justice (2.6b–3.18). The heading of courage, of course, belongs to the martyrs, together with the virtue of piety: although frequently subsumed under the heading of justice, piety can also appear in lists of the cardinal virtues in place of 'prudence' or 'rational judgment' (which, as we have seen, can be a sort of root virtue for the rest).

Looking back to 1.3-4 in the *exordium*, one can see that some textual corruption may indeed have occurred: 1.3 speaks of the passions that hinder self control, giving as examples the very passions (gluttony and lust) that are taken up in 1.31-2.6; 1.4a speaks of the passions that inhibit justice, giving only malice as an example and introducing anger, together with fear and pain, under the emotions that hinder courage. Anger would be better placed as a threat to justice, as indeed it appears in 2.16-20. Fear and pain are appropriate as antagonists of courage, but anger does not fit.

Mastery of Passions that Hinder Self Control
Self control was widely recognized as an important virtue, and writers on ethics frequently highlighted its essential role in securing virtue. Elevation of the passions to the rank of 'chief antagonist' of virtue led, on the one hand, to an elevation of prudence (rational judgment) as the cornerstone of the virtues, since it represented the power of reason to choose virtue over vice; on the other hand, this focus on the passions brought greater attention to self control, the taming of the passions by means of reason (cf. Aristotle, *On Virtues and Vices* 5.1; Cicero, *Tusculun Disputations* 4.22; Plato, *Gorgias* 507C). *4 Macc.* 1.31 shares this basic definition of self control (1.30b-31), but as proof of reason's dominion over the passions by means of self control the author looks to the loyal observance of the dietary regulations of the Torah, the prohibitions against certain kinds of food (seafood: Lev. 11.9-12; Deut. 14.9-10; fowl: Lev. 11.13-23; Deut. 14.11-20; quadrupeds: Lev. 11.4-8; Deut.

14.4-8; swarming creatures: Lev. 11.41-42; animals that die of themselves: Deut. 14.21). The author thus shares with the author of the *Letter of Aristeas* and Philo an interest in explaining the benefits of keeping
the commands of the Torah, especially the most ethnically particular
laws (dietary regulations and the like), in terms of Greek ethical philosophy. All three authors share an insistence that a moralizing or allego-
rizing reading of the laws does not replace the literal observance of
them. The very observance of these dietary laws which elicits ridicule
and slander from many Gentiles (cf. Tacitus, *Histories* 5.4.3; Juvenal,
Satires 14.98-99; Josephus, *Apion* 2.137) becomes the demonstration.
The author, in using the first person plural ('when *we* crave...*we*
abstain', 1.34), has very astutely involved his hearers. Their own observance of dietary laws becomes a proof of reason's upper hand in their
lives, and hence a cause for self respect and pride. He does not yet give
reasons for keeping the Torah's dietary regulations (as he will in 5.22-
26): the mere fact of keeping them demonstrates the virtue of self control. This is a significant rejoinder to dominant cultural criticism,
comparable to what one finds, for example, in Philo (*Spec. Leg.* 4.100).

A second example of reason gaining the upper hand by means of self
control offers itself in the story of Joseph, tempted by the wife of
Potiphar (Gen. 39.7-12). Joseph became well known as a model of
temperance, a virtue that is repeatedly celebrated in the *Testament of
Joseph*. Despite the power of sexual desire, and despite the fact that,
given his stage of physical development, he was most naturally suited to
yield to those suggestions, Joseph refused to wrong his patron (his master Potiphar) and violate the sanctity of the marriage bed. Joseph's
example proves that reason can master desire. At this point, the author
cites the last prohibition of the Decalogue: the very fact that the Law
prohibits covetousness, he claims, proves that reason can master covetousness. This is a very different understanding from what one finds in
Paul (Rom 7.7-24). Here it is assumed that the Law commands what is
possible, not what is impossible, and so careful observance of the Law is
an adequate guide to overcome the 'passions of the flesh' (contra Paul
in Gal 5.16-25). The importance of this commandment is noted also by
Philo, who sees desire (covetousness) as the sole passion that undermines the person from within, whereas all other passions 'attack the
soul from without' (*Dec.* 142-143; cf. *Spec. Leg.* 4.84).

Mastery of Passions that Hinder Justice
The author moves on in 2.6b to show how reason masters the 'emotions
that hinder one from justice'. Despite the lack of textual support, I

would suggest that 2.7 has been misplaced: it would round out the discussion of self control quite well, where topics of gluttony and lust have
already been treated; the form of the verse also functions as a support for
the claim made in 2.6a, but hardly for the statement in 2.6b. 2.8-9, however, does provide support for 2.6b, and the claim that the passions that
hinder the expression of justice can be overcome. Again the author looks
to the Torah as the guide: 'as soon as one adopts a way of life in accordance with the law', he or she is forced to act justly. Here the specific
commands are presented as a sort of exercise or training, building up the
reasoning faculty's ability to choose what is just, and beating down the
selfish impulses that move people to violate justice.

Greed and love of money are the passions targeted in the author's
first examples. While love of money might make one set financial gain
above social relationships and dealing with fellow Jews according to
God's standards, the Torah commands that money be lent to the poor
within the community without interest (Exod. 22.25; Deut. 23.19-20)
and that all debts be cancelled in the seventh year. There has been
some discussion as to whether the sabbatical (Deut. 15.1-2, 9) or
jubilee year (Lev. 25.8-17) is intended by the author. Both share the
common points that God, as the founder and patron of the community, has the right to regulate that community's business, that desire for
gain is not to take precedence over group solidarity and mutual assistance, and that no part of a community set free by God is to become
enslaved again to another part of that community through debt and
perpetual indenture. The Greek suggests that the sabbatical year is
specifically in mind. The prohibitions against gleaning the field and
gathering up the last of the grapes (Exod. 23.10-11; Lev. 19.9-10),
which provide a sort of welfare for the poor who come to glean (Ruth
2.2-3), also cause one to choose justice over greed. In all of these
examples, the role of the Torah is becoming more and more important.

Through dedication to carry out the commands of the Torah, reason
can even rule the generally positive passions of parental, filial and con-
jugal affection, so that one places virtue above any of these relationships, especially by disciplining children and bringing them up in the
ways of the law (cf. e.g. Deut. 21.18-21; Prov. 13.23; 19.18). The
author subsequently gives a highly moving example of this claim as he
considers how the seven brothers mastered fraternal affection
(13.19–14.1), and the mother mastered affection for offspring (14.13-
20; 15.23-28), for the sake of piety. These natural affections would
have caused them to preserve their lives for one another, but, because

they were wholly ruled by reason (led by the Torah), they did not capitulate to the tyrant in order to preserve their natural family.

Just as reason can overcome the hesitancy of familial love and friendship to rebuke or correct transgression (2.10-13), so it can, through following the Torah, also overcome the passions of enmity (2.14). The one who lives by the law will not destroy the crops of the enemy even in the midst of war (Deut. 20.19-20), and will not stand by while the enemy's property is jeopardized, but will help preserve it (Exod. 23.4-5; Deut. 22.4). Reference to commandments that promote 'love of the enemy' served to answer the primary criticism levelled against Jews by representatives of the dominant culture, namely that the Jews cared for one another but expended no effort to help those of other races (Tacitus, *Histories* 5.5; Josephus, *Apion* 2.121; Diodorus of Sicily 34/35.1.1-2). Diodorus specifically claimed that the Torah itself is a body of xenophobic laws (34/35.1.4). The author of *4 Maccabees*, like Philo, the author of the *Letter of Aristeas* and Josephus, denies such claims, showing instead that the Torah promotes a humanitarian demeanour towards all people, friend or enemy, Jew or Gentile. By stressing this type of commandment, the author reminds his hearers to continue to seek to do good to their critics, to undermine their criticism by acting benevolently .

After declaring that reason masters a broad range of 'violent emotions' (recalling the malevolent tendency of pleasure in the soul in 1.25-26), the author looks at how reason should be expected to master anger (2.15-20). Moses provides the first example, which is taken from Num. 16.1-35. Korah, Kohath, Dathan and Abiram rebelled against the leadership of Moses and Aaron, asserting that they enjoyed no special holiness or commission from God. Moses was angered by this outrage to his leadership and affront to his honour, but did not act out of his anger. The author's point is that, rather than take vengeance against his opponents himself (the natural aim of anger in Aristotle's definition in *Rhetoric* 2.2.1), he submitted the matter to God, to whom alone belongs judgment and vengeance. He acted justly, since he did not arrogate to himself what belongs to God. The example of Moses is strikingly similar to that of Achilles in Plutarch (*How to Study Poetry* 8 [*Moralia* 26E]): Achilles was about to commit murder not for honour or advantage, but out of anger: 'although he could not altogether eradicate his anger, yet before doing anything irreparable he put it aside and checked it by making it obedient to his reason'.

The second example is a negative one, the full story of which can be found in Gen. 34.1-31. To avenge the defiling of their sister Dinah (Gen. 34.13), Simeon and Levi carried out a deceitful plan to slaughter the males of the city of Shechem. Jacob's words in his deathbed speech, 'cursed be their anger' (Gen. 49.7), were an allusion to this irrational action. Simeon and Levi failed to control their anger, and to accept some means of reconciliation. The author's point here is simply that, if anger were not under reason's jurisdiction, and if it were not possible for reason to control anger, Jacob would not have censured their anger on his deathbed.

The author now returns to an objection raised as early as 1.5-6. Reason cannot be expected to master its own emotions and passions, namely forgetfulness and ignorance, but only those of the body (the author should add, too, the passions of the soul). Forgetfulness and ignorance were widely classified as passions, but these are not of the sort that reason is expected to master. Indeed, Philo does not appear to attach any degree of culpability to succumbing to these, 'for forgetfulness is not a voluntary affection, but is one of those things which are not actually in us, but which come upon us from without' (*Migr. Abr.* 206). The author leaves this topic rather undeveloped, turning instead to support his earlier claim that reason does not extirpate, but only regulates, the passions:

> No one of us can eradicate that kind of desire [the passions of the body (or soul)], but reason can provide a way for us not to be enslaved by desire. No one of us can eradicate anger from the mind, but reason can help to deal with anger. No one of us can eradicate malice, but reason can fight at our side so that we are not overcome by malice. For reason does not uproot the emotions but is their antagonist (*4 Macc.* 3.2-5).

Here the impossibility (rather than inexpediency) of destroying the passions is stressed. Philo would disagree with the author of *4 Maccabees* here at one point: for Philo, Moses, the figure of the 'perfect man', is able to extirpate the passions (particularly anger); it is the aim of Aaron, the figure of the next-to-perfect man, to control and temper the passions so that they do not gain the upper hand (*Leg. All.* 3.129-32). Philo, however, reserved for Moses a special distinction, and agreed that most people would do well to match Aaron's achievement.

The one who seeks virtue is thus called to resist the tendency of the passions to lead one into vicious acts or pursuits, to be vigilant and to prevent oneself from committing some impiety or injustice or failing to act justly and courageously when the circumstances call for such action.

Reason—the devout reason that has been trained by and is continually led by the Torah—can ensure the victory of virtue. This seemingly academic clarification is not without substantial pastoral comfort. If it is accepted that God requires only mastery, not extirpation, of the passions, many would no longer drive themselves to distraction with self-inflicted guilt for every wrong desire, nor, indeed, for every licit pleasure.

The example with which the author supports his position is the story of King David's thirst, taken from 2 Sam. 23.13-17//1 Chron. 11.15-19. Townshend (1913: 670) suggests that 'either his Bible differed materially from ours, or else he allowed himself considerable latitude in handling the incident'. The latter seems the more likely possibility, given both the lack of any manuscript witness to such a different text of 2 Samuel and the latitude the author employed with his historical sources for the Hellenization crisis and the martyr narratives. A cursory glance at the biblical source will reveal the major differences: *4 Macc.* 3.7-9 has no counterpart in 2 Samuel; the three soldiers become two young soldiers in *4 Macc.* 3.12; *4 Maccabees* adds mention of the soldiers' motives in fulfilling the king's desire.

Affected by the passion of thirst following a long day's campaign, David conceived an irrational longing for the water in the territory held by the enemy. It is this irrational longing that is the danger to virtue, which sought not just the slaking of the thirst (which could have been done from the springs in David's camp, and hence from God's provision), but the slaking of it in a way that was not feasible without great danger and loss (roving beyond God's provision). Two young soldiers risked their lives to steal into the enemy camp and bring back some water for the king, 'but David, although he was burning with thirst, considered it an altogether fearful danger to his soul to drink what was regarded as equivalent to blood. Therefore, opposing reason to desire, he poured out the drink as an offering to God' (3.15-16).

Klauck (1989a: 702) believes that the prohibition against consuming blood (Lev. 17.11-14) is the explanation for David's action, since the water was brought at the risk of human life ('equivalent to blood'). A more likely explanation, however, is to be found in the fear of *hubris*, provoking God by claiming more than is due to a mortal. David realized that the water was too valuable to be spent on a physical passion of a human being, so he decided on an act that would be more appropriate to the value of the drink. David's pouring out of the water as a drink offering—not an act of atonement with the 'blood' but a gesture showing that the drink was worth more than a mortal deserved—was an act of justice, giving to God what was due to God and not arrogating for a mortal more than was due to a mortal. Aeschylus's *Agamemnon* provides an informative parallel. After returning home 'victorious' from Troy, Clytemnestra invites the king to tread upon a runner of scarlet linens from his chariot into his house. Agamemnon has strong scruples about daring to accept such an honour:

> Draw not down envy upon my path by strewing it with tapestries. 'Tis the gods we must honour thus; but for a mortal to tread upon broidered fineries is, to my judgement, not without ground for dread. I bid thee revere me not as a god, but as a man' (*Agamemnon* 920-25).

When he did consent to Clytemnestra's request, he prayed: 'As I tread upon these purple vestments may I not be smitten from afar by any glance of Heaven's jealous eye. Sore shame it is for my foot to mar the substance of the house by making waste of wealth and costly woven work' (*Agamemnon* 943-47). While Agamemnon failed to act in accordance with justice, respecting what was due the gods and arrogating none of those privileges, David did act in accordance with justice, 'for the temperate mind can conquer the drives of the emotions and quench the flames of frenzied desires' (3.17). This example confirms the author's position in that David was still thirsty after he 'opposed reason to desire'. He did not extirpate his passion, but rather did not permit it to lead him to sin against God.

Mastery of Passions that hinder Courage, Piety and Wisdom
All of this has served as a preamble to the author's presentation of his primary exemplars of his thesis, namely the martyrs Eleazar, the seven brothers, and their mother. These figures are associated by the author chiefly with the virtues of courage, piety (an aspect of justice, giving to God what is God's due) and wisdom, and with not permitting the passions of physical pain, fear, or even natural affection to hinder the perfect expression of those virtues. The author presented these figures in far greater detail than the earlier examples of Joseph, Moses, or David, but this is due to the threefold purpose that they serve. Their examples were proofs of his thesis; their noble achievements formed the basis of accolades that would rouse emulation among the hearers; their conversations would become the basis for the audience's own deliberations about the way of life it would choose amidst the pressures it faced.

The author sets the stage by recounting the Hellenizing 'revolution' in Palestine under the high priest Jason and the onslaught of divine

chastisement in the form of the suppression of Torah-observance under
Antiochus IV (3.20-4.26). Antiochus begins to enforce this policy by
gathering together a number of the inhabitants of Jerusalem with the
intention of forcing them under the threat of torture and execution to
eat pork as a sign of their willingness to relinquish their ancestral customs in favour of the Greek way of life (5.1-3). The first Jew to be
brought forward is Eleazar, an aged priest and respected elder (5.4).
Antiochus seeks to persuade Eleazar to renounce his 'foolish philosophy' (5.5-13), but Eleazar vigorously defends the keeping of the Torah
(5.14-32). Like Socrates, who refused to violate his life of virtue, now
near its end, in order to save it shamefully (cf. Epictetus, *Discourses*
4.1.163-165; Plato, *Crito* 52A-54C), so Eleazar declares that he will not
now violate his native law for the sake of a few more years (5.32-38).
Like Socrates, he seeks to preserve not his life, but the lawfulness of his
life and the virtues that he had striven to cultivate throughout that long
life. In refusing to break faith with the Torah (a violation of justice, cf.
Cicero, *Rhetorica ad Herennium,* 3.3.4) and renounce his self control,
Eleazar repeats Socrates' resolution 'to live and die in the practice alike
of justice and of all other virtue' (Plato, *Gorgias* 527E).

In the scene that follows, Eleazar is tortured with flagellation,
beaten, and eventually tormented by fiery instruments, giving the
author an opportunity to demonstrate that 'devout reason' masters even
external agonies (6.31-35). The physical pain is seen as a more compelling and stronger 'emotion' than greed or lust, but Eleazar will not
be compelled by these agonies to play the coward and break faith with
his ancestral law (6.19-21). Rather, 'he bore the pains and scorned the
punishment and endured the tortures' (6.9), proving that the Jewish
philosophy is a credible way of life (7.9), making possible the things
that the author promises (i.e. mastery of the emotions). 'Despising
hardships' was a familiar topic in Stoic and Cynic philosophical discourse. Dio Chrysostom (*Orations* 8.18), for example, urged the
philosopher to approach hardships boldly and with an air of contempt,
for this would make them easier to master. In this same oration, the
philosopher who wrestles with hardships, the most 'difficult of antagonists', is likened to an athlete. Unlike those who compete for a mere
sprig of a tree, however, the philosopher competes for the greatest
prize—virtue. In this same sense, Eleazar is presented as a 'noble athlete' (6.10), and athletic imagery becomes one of the dominant
metaphors for interpreting the martyrs' struggle.

Eleazar is victorious because he can endure as much or more than the torturers can inflict (6.10; cf. 1.11). This is another familiar image from Stoic ethical philosophy. Philo, for example, writes:

> I have observed in a contest of pancratiasts how one of the combatants will strike blow after blow with his hands and feet, every one of them well aimed, and leave nothing undone that might secure his victory, and yet he will finally quit the arena without a crown in a state of exhaustion and collapse, while the object of his attack, a mass of closely packed flesh, rigid and solid, full of the wiriness of the true athlete, his sinews taut from end to end, firm as a piece of rock or iron, will yield not a whit to the blows, but by his stark and stubborn endurance will break down utterly the strength of his adversary and end by winning a complete victory. Much the same as it seems to me is the case of the virtuous man; his soul strongly fortified with a resolution firmly founded on reason, he compels the employer of violence to give up in exhaustion, sooner than himself submit to do anything contrary to his judgement (*Omn. Prob. Lib.* 26-27; cf. Seneca, *De constantia sapientis* 9.4).

Eleazar triumphed, not because he avoided pain, but because pain could not overcome his commitment to virtue. It is not mere stubbornness that motivates the Jewish martyrs, however—the author points to their hope as the pillar of their endurance. Eleazar, and indeed all who 'attend to religion with a whole heart' and 'believe that they ... do not die to God, but live to God' (7.18-19) are able to rise above the passion of physical pain when it challenges their loyalty to God and God's law.

The second scene of martyrdom involves the seven brothers who were tortured one after the other, but who preferred to die and encourage one another to remain steadfast rather than give way to cowardice and fear, on the one hand, and to the prospect of temporal advantage, on the other hand. As with Eleazar, so here also Antiochus seeks to persuade the brothers to renounce their dedication to Torah-observance. He offers both the threat of more extreme torture (8.2, 11-14) and the enticement of preferment and power at the king's court (8.3-10). Rather than yield to the emotion of fear or the prospect of pleasure, which would lead them to act in a cowardly and impious manner, they also resolve to die rather than transgress their ancestral law (9.1). Safety through transgression (i.e. dishonourable means) is more grievous to them than pain and death (9.4), a statement which recalls the topic of courage, namely, preferring death to any safety gained at the cost of a disgraceful retreat (Aristotle, *Nicomachean Ethics* 3.8.3 [1116b19-22]; Tacitus, *Agricola* 34). Such transgression of the

Torah would rob the youths of the 'prize of virtue', and so, like
Socrates, they prefer to renounce the honours that excite the majority
of people and live for virtue (Plato, *Gorgias* 526d-527b).

The brothers recall, for Antiochus's benefit, the example of Eleazar,
which should have taught the tyrant that his mission was futile and
doomed to failure. Eleazar had already shown that devout reason can
overcome the tyrant who threatens from outside, who cannot by
means of physical agonies shackle and dominate the reason of the loyal
Jew (cf. the frequent references to this theme in Epictetus, *Discourses*
1.29.5-8; 1.18.17). Eleazar's ability to maintain the duties of piety 'while
enduring torture', the brothers claim, has instructed them concerning
their duty as well (9.6). They boldly challenge Antiochus to put their
commitment to the test, knowing that death at his hands would be a
'splendid favour' (11.12) since it enables the brothers to attain the
height of virtue and receive the reward of immortality more speedily
(9.8; 14.5).

In the scenes that follow, the author displays his mastery of the
rhetorical technique of 'vivid description' (*ekphrasis*), exercised here not
to offend the sensibilities of the audience but to heighten their appreciation of the martyrs' endurance through the vivid, chilling depiction of
their sufferings. This contributes to the author's portrayal of the
extreme case that ought to facilitate resistance and steadfastness in the
audience's more moderate difficulties. As he describes in detail the
physical torments to which the brothers were subjected, the audience
can better appreciate the strength of the 'devout reason' that can master
such agonies.

The oldest brother expresses well this contest between pain and reason when he, like Eleazar, refuses to be released from the tortures
through transgression of the Torah: 'your wheel is not so powerful as
to strangle my reason' (9.17). He asserts the 'freedom of the wise man':
as with the ideal sage of Stoic and Cynic ethical discourses, the young
man's upright reason (*orthos logos*, 1.15; 6.7) cannot be made to bend
through assaults on the body. Rather, in the midst of torments, the second brother may even claim to experience the 'joys that come from
virtue' (9.31) as he remains firm in his commitment to piety. It is the
tyrant who suffers worse pains, according to this youth, because he
cannot compel them even through his most ingenious devices to act
contrary to their devout reason (9.30). Similarly, the fourth brother
professes the powerlessness of physical assaults to reach the pious person's
mind and turn his reason away from the path of virtue: 'You do not

have a fire hot enough to make me play the coward' (10.14; cf. 10.17).

Following the death of the seventh brother, the author returns to his thesis in a paragraph very similar to that which followed Eleazar's martyrdom (6.31-35). The triumph of the youths over pains affords incontrovertible proof that devout reason can master the passions (13.1). They were not 'slaves to their emotions', such that they gave in to them and consented to depart from virtue, but rather exercised the complete freedom of the philosopher. Philo gave a clear definition of this metaphorical use of freedom and slavery in philosophical discourse:

> Slavery then is applied in one sense to bodies, in another to souls; bodies have men for their masters, souls their vices and passions. The same is true of freedom; one freedom produces security of the body from men of superior strength, the other sets the mind at liberty from the domination of the passions (*Omn. Prob. Lib.* 17).

Slavery was considered to be a disgraceful state; it was far more disgraceful, according to the philosophers, to be slaves inwardly to one's own passions and tendencies toward vice. The seven brothers, like their aged instructor, were tainted with no such disgrace.

The author introduces into his discussion of the triumph of the brothers' reason over the emotions the topic of fraternal affection—a particularly strong kinship bond that formed another emotional obstacle for the 'athletes of virtue' to overcome. Much of what one finds in *4 Maccabees* on this topic can be found also in Plutarch ('On Fraternal Affection', *Moralia* 478-90) and in Aristotle (*Nicomachean Ethics* 8.12 [1161b11-62a34]), who considered fraternal affection a form of friendship. Fraternal affection was 'implanted in the mother's womb' (*4 Macc.* 13.19), nourished by being 'shaped during the same period of time, growing from the same blood and through the same life' (13.20), taking 'milk from the same fountains' (13.21), and made stronger from this 'common nurture and daily companionship, and from both general education and our discipline in the law of God' (13.22). *4 Maccabees* shares all these particulars with Plutarch and Xenophon (*Cyropaedia* 8.7, 14), except for the last item, which introduces the distinctively Jewish element in the brothers' training. This training in the Law actualizes the Aristotelian ideal of friendship among the brothers (*Nicomachean Ethics* 1156b6-7: 'Perfect friendship is the friendship of people who are good and alike in virtue'), for they share a 'common zeal for nobility' (*kalokagathia*, the term describing the Greek ideal citizen, 13.25).

Although a positive emotion, fraternal affection is still an emotion— one over which reason must be master. The author has affirmed that the Torah even trained its devotees to place considerations of virtue higher than considerations of natural, positive affections (2.10-13), and here gives the audience a potent proof of his claim:

See Plut.

> But although nature and companionship and virtuous habits had augmented the affection of family [sibling] ties, those who were left endured for the sake of religion, while watching their brothers being maltreated and tortured to death. Furthermore, they encouraged them to face the torture, so that they not only despised their agonies, but also mastered the emotions of brotherly love (13.27–14.1).

Klauck (1990: 155) notes that 'for the sake of brotherly love the seven brothers would have had to save their lives for one another's sake by eating meat offered to idols'. Rather, they endure 'what is more grievous than death' (Plutarch, 'On the Bravery of Women' [*Moralia* 253D-E]), namely watching one another die. Like the two sisters who, in Plutarch's story, help one another commit suicide rather than face rape and execution, the brothers instruct one another on dying nobly rather than submit to disgrace, overcoming the pain of watching a sibling die in order that each brother might receive eternal benefit. Again, the brothers fulfil Aristotle's ideal of virtuous friendship: 'being true to themselves, these also remain true to one another, and neither request nor render services that are morally degrading. Indeed, they may be said actually to restrain each other from evil: since good men neither err themselves nor permit their friends to err' (*Nicomachean Ethics* 8.8.5 [1159b3-7]).

The behaviour of the brothers as true friends cannot fail to have had an impact on the audience. 'Fictive kinship' was common in philosophical schools, where all people were regarded as 'brothers and sisters', and especially strong, for example, in the Pythagorean school (cf. Plutarch, 'On Fraternal Affection' 17 [*Moralia* 488B-C]). This phenomenon also took strong hold in the early Christian community. Jews, however, had readier access to using such kinship language to articulate their relationship and obligations to one another, for they shared a common ancestor: 'Abraham is our father' (Jn 8.39). The representative nature of the brothers and the symbolic nature of the number seven should have made it an easy step for the audience to see their own obligations in the story of the seven brothers. As Klauck (1990: 155) rightly observes, the harmony of the brothers (13.25; 14.3-8) echoes the 'ideal state of the whole Jewish people (3.21)'. The Jewish community as a whole is to exercise 'harmony' and agreement (14.3, 6-7), unified around their common training in the Torah. Moreover, they are called to act as virtuous friends, urging one another to eschew baseness (capitulation) and remain steadfast in virtue (commitment to the Torah). Like brothers and sisters, who are also friends, they must not allow one another to go wrong, and for the sake of one another must not go wrong themselves.

The final and climactic inductive proof for this 'narrative demonstration' is the mother of the seven brothers, who demonstrates the mastery of devout reason over the passions in a way that stands above and beyond the endurance and firmness of men (15.30). The principal emotion that the mother has to master is maternal love. The author draws extensively from popular philosophy for his material, and once more there is a parallel for every point in Plutarch ('On Affection for Offspring' [*Moralia* 493B-496A]) and Aristotle (*Nicomachean Ethics* 8.12.2-3 [1161b20-28]). Like Plutarch, he turns to the examples of animals (even the same animals—birds—are featured) in order to show the characteristic of parental affection (*philostorgia*). Plutarch explains why examples from animals are useful for the exploration of such subjects (*Moralia* 493C): 'in dumb animals Nature preserves their special characteristics pure and unmixed and simple, but in human beings, through reason and habit, they have been modified by many opinions and adventitious judgements so that they have lost their proper form'. Animal behaviour provides the key to perceiving what is 'natural' and 'pure', thus what parental love 'according to nature' might look like. *4 Maccabees* notes that protection is a major function of parental love, shown both in the building of nests in safe places and in the willingness of both birds and bees to risk their own lives so that their offspring may escape the hunter (14.15-19; cf. Plutarch, *Moralia* 494A-E).

Further, parental affection is increased by the likeness of the children and parents in both body and soul (15.4), a feature frequently noted by Stoic philosophers especially. Hadas (1953: 220) cites a striking parallel from Nemesius, *De natura hominum*: 'Cleanthes...declares that we are similar to our parents not only in respect to body but also in respect to soul, in emotions, morals, dispositions' (cf. also Plutarch, *Plac. Philos.* 7.11.3 [quoted in Hadas 1953: 220]). Likeness, for Aristotle, was the essence of friendship and affection: the mother and her seven sons shared not only physical likeness, but also likeness of soul, constitution and values, all having been trained in the same Torah. The power of the *pathos* of parental affection is heightened here precisely because it is the mother who witnesses the pain of the children. Again it is a commonplace in the ancient world that the mother feels more strongly for her children than does the father (Aristotle, *Nicomachean Ethics* 8.12.3 [1161b27-28]; Euripides, *Frag.* 1015), attributed by our author to their suffering of the birthpangs on behalf of the children (15.4, 7).

Despite the power of such natural 'sympathy' and the 'tender love' planted in her by nature itself (15.6-7; cf. Plutarch, *Moralia* 496A), the mother's reason did not falter in the contest, for 'she was of the same mind as Abraham' (14.20), who is known in this discourse especially for his willingness to give up the life of his son for the sake of obedience to the divine command (13.12; 16.20; 18.11). In order to make the mother's endurance more real and impressive, the author exercises all his skill in *ekphrasis*, 'vivid description', in 15.12-22, making the sufferings of the seven children as vivid as possible, implanting on the audience the sense-impressions that struck the mother with overwhelming force. Just as the brothers conquered the emotion of fraternal affection (*philadelphia*), so the mother is able to control the power of parental affection (*philostorgia*): 'though so many factors influenced the mother to suffer with them out of love for her children, in the case of none of them were the various tortures strong enough to pervert her reason' (15.11).

The author portrays the mother as acting in accordance with wisdom, weighing advantages and disadvantages correctly (cf. *Rhetorica ad Herennium* 3.3.4). 'Faith in God' (15.24) was the ultimate source of her choice, for this firmness toward God opened up the considerations of temporal versus eternal advantage:

> Two courses were open to this mother, that of religion, and that of preserving her seven sons for a time, as the tyrant had promised. She loved religion more, the religion that preserves them for eternal life according to God's promise...because of the fear of God she disdained the temporary safety of her children... For as in the council chamber of her own soul she saw mighty advocates—nature, family, parental love, and the rackings of her children—this mother held two ballots, one bearing death and the other deliverance for her children. She did not approve the deliverance that would preserve the seven sons for a short time, but as the daughter of God-fearing Abraham she remembered his fortitude (15.2-3, 8, 25-28).

The mother, reasoning according to piety and the assurance that God would be faithful to God's loyal clients, understood that temporary safety, which rested on the tyrant's promise, could only be purchased at the cost of 'eternal life according to God's promise' (15.3). Indeed, she realized that the result of seeking safety now through transgression would result in danger before God's court. 'Fear of God' (15.8) properly motivates her to steadfastness as it did the seven brothers (13.14-15). The author paints a vivid picture of the 'council chamber' within the mother's soul, where the advocates of 'nature, family, parental love, and the rackings of her children' proclaimed their loud testimony. Bravely, she cast the ballot for death now, rather than preserve them for a brief span only to lose them for eternity.

Her wisdom enables the mother not to be fainthearted in the face of such grievous loss or of the onslaught of emotions. The author introduces a 'fainthearted' speech, which his exemplar did not actually give, in order to provide a vivid contrast for her truly courageous response:

> O how wretched am I and many times unhappy! After bearing seven children, I am now the mother of none! O seven childbirths all in vain, seven profitless pregnancies, fruitless nurturings and wretched nursings! In vain, my sons, I endured many birth pangs for you, and the more grievous anxieties of your upbringing. Alas for my children, some unmarried, others married and without off-spring. I shall not see your children or have the happiness of being called grandmother. Alas, I who had so many and beautiful children am a widow and alone, with many sorrows. And when I die, I shall have none of my sons to bury me (16.6-11).

Such a lament would be familiar indeed to any audience with exposure to Greek drama, which may be compared point for point with similar laments in Euripides' *Trojan Women* or *Suppliant Maidens*. After her little son is condemned by the Greeks to die, Andromache cries out: 'In vain and all in vain this breast…hath nurtured thee. Vainly I travailed and was spent with toils!' (*Trojan Women* 758-760; cf. 380-381). Hecuba, whose sons have all been killed and whose daughters have all been apportioned out as spoils, laments: 'Nor son nor daughter, none remains to help the wretched mother, of all born to her' (*Trojan Women* 504-505); for those Trojans deprived of their children, 'none remain to spill earth's blood-gift [i.e. pour libations] at their tombs' (*Trojan Women* 382).

Why should the author evaluate such a lament as unbecoming to this 'God-fearing' mother (16.12), as showing a faint heart? Such grief or lamenting would, in fact, contradict the mother's estimation of advantage and undermine the credibility of her choice, as if dying for religion were not ultimately the most beneficial course for her children. Having confidence in God's power and favour, she knows that her pregnancies were not profitless: by urging her sons on to die for God's

Torah, she is not losing them but rather 'giving rebirth for immortality to the whole number of her sons' (16.13). She, like Eleazar, is fully convinced that 'those who die for the sake of God live to God' (16.25; cf. 7.19), and therefore does not grieve as if over the lost.

The author once again brings the example directly back into the thesis of the whole (16.1-4). Like Eleazar and the seven brothers, so the mother 'quenched so many and such great emotions by devout reason' (16.4) and rendered his thesis incontrovertible. What the author has truly demonstrated, however, is not merely the philosophical thesis but the specifically Jewish interpretation of that thesis, namely that the mind which is fully subject to the Torah is able to exercise mastery over every passion (those which are recognized as vicious, but also those which are natural and generally positive) and so remain steadfast in virtue.

Conclusion

In the philosophical aspect of his discourse, the author has already made a remarkable achievement. He has given to the keeping of the Jewish Torah the status of an ethical philosophy dedicated to fulfiling the highest ideals of virtue. The author has discussed at length how following the way of the Torah brought one's life into harmony with the virtues of self control, justice, courage, piety, and wisdom. While non-Jews may not recognize this equivalence, his audience surely will, and it will help them maintain their self-respect without compromising their Jewish identity or their loyalty to God's covenant. Does one seek virtue, and the honour that accompanies it? Does one seek to establish the rule of reason over the passions that hinder this quest? Jews already possess the most reliable guide and instructor—the Law which is the essence of Wisdom. As they continue to give themselves to its instruction they can be assured that they, like the martyrs, will be exemplars of virtue and the highest nobility (1.8, 10).

Further Reading

Philosophical Content of 4 Maccabees
Most scholars would agree that the author of *4 Maccabees* did not align himself with any particular philosophical school, but rather benefited from a number of philosophical influences, especially Platonism and Stoicism. Important primary texts for the investigation of Stoic ethical philosophy include Cicero, *Tusculan Disputations*, Epictetus, *Discourses* and *Encheiridion* (or, *Manual*), Seneca, *Ad Lucil-*

ium Epistulae Morales (*Moral Epistles*) and *Moral Essays*. Especially helpful as a parallel to *4 Maccabees* is Seneca's *De constantia sapientis*, 'On the Firmness of the Wise Person'. Redditt (1983) explores the author's use of Stoic conceptions to demonstrate the value of the Torah as revelation of the way in which to live in accordance with the divine world order and as educator in rational living. Renehan (1972) argues cogently for the diversity of opinion within Stoicism and the likelihood of Posidonius' influence upon the author of *4 Maccabees*, specifically concerning the role of reason as the governor rather than the destroyer of the emotions and passions. Breitenstein (1978: 132-79) examines the Platonic and Stoic influences on the author of *4 Maccabees*, together with a perhaps too negative assessment of the author's philosophical ability and innovation.

Fraternal and Parental Affection
Klauck (1990) offers a fine discussion of the connections between *4 Maccabees* and popular philosophical discussion of fraternal affection. Important primary sources for this topic are Plutarch, 'On Fraternal Affection', and Aristotle, *Nicomachean Ethics*, Books 8 and 9. While the latter is chiefly a discussion of friendship, it contains lengthy passages on fraternal affection as a form of friendship. Plutarch, 'On the Bravery of Women' and 'On Affection for Offspring', offers useful comparative material on parental affection and on female displays of courage.

Quotations from Cicero, Plutarch, Aristotle, Diogenes Laertius, Epictetus, Seneca, Euripides, Plato and Aeschylus are taken from the LCL editions; quotations from Philo, *Quod omnis probum liber sit*, are taken from the LCL edition; all other quotations from Philo are taken from the revised edition of Yonge's translation.

4

4 *MACCABEES* AS ENCOMIUM

The stories of the endurance of Eleazar, the seven brothers, and their mother serve in the first instance as inductive proofs of the philosophical thesis, but we have seen above in Chapter 2 that examples in the context of an epideictic speech do not function merely as proofs. While the examples confirm that devout reason can indeed master the passions, the laudatory handling of these figures will have the rhetorical effect of rousing emulation within the hearers, leading them to imitate the heroic commitment to virtue seen in these exemplars. Aristotle and other rhetorical theorists noted that 'praise and counsels have a common aspect', since what one praises is generally what one would advise and vice versa (*Rhetoric* 1.9.35-36; Quintilian, *Institutes* 3.7.28). Pseudo-Cicero observes further that, while virtue is itself desirable, 'if it can be shown that praise accrues, the desire to strive after the right is doubled' (*Rhetorica ad Herennium* 3.4.7). The 'praise' of the martyrs (1.10) that the author proposes as fitting to the occasion will promote their way of life and their commitment to it as desirable in the eyes of his audience.

The choice of exemplars and the manner of their presentation are highly significant. The author's choice of the martyrs under Antiochus as the *best* exemplars of the mastery of reason over the passions spoke directly to the audience's situation. These martyrs refused even for the sake of life to depart from the instructions of the Torah, but rather defended the viability and value of the Jewish way of life with their own blood. Singular commitment to the Torah and the achievement of virtue and a praiseworthy remembrance are thus directly connected. Moreover, the shameful death of the martyrs—the outcome of the dominant culture's negative evaluation of their way of life—is completely transformed in the author's presentation into a noble death. These martyrs did not die on account of 'madness' or failure to appreciate the good things of life (cf. 8.5, 8), but rather on account of 'virtue' (*aretē*, 1.8) and highest 'nobility' (*kalokagathia*, 1.10). These two Greek terms, which elsewhere sum up the Greek ideal of the virtuous person, are here applied to those who resisted Hellenization where it compromised their loyalty to the Jewish Law. The highest terms of praise within the dominant culture thus come to be applied to those who most firmly resist assimilation into that culture and preserve the Jewish way of life.

The Dynamics of Encomia

The encomium, or laudatory speech, was an important means of reaffirming assent to a society's central values. These speeches, frequently commemorative addresses for the dead (akin to the modern eulogy), praised their subjects by showing how they led a life closely in line with the Greek ideals of virtue and happiness. The purpose was not merely to honour the subjects of the speech, but to renew dedication among the hearers to the virtues that the fallen embodied. Hearing another praised was expected to rouse the emotion of emulation in the hearer. Aristotle (*Rhetoric* 2.11.1) defines emulation as

> a feeling of pain at the evident presence of highly valued goods, which are possible for us to attain, in the possession of those who naturally resemble us—pain not due to the fact that another possesses them, but to the fact that we ourselves do not. Emulation therefore is virtuous and characteristic of virtuous men…for [he], owing to emulation, fits himself to obtain such goods.

The one who felt emulation would prepare himself or herself to attain the same honour and favourable remembrance by following the virtuous course seen in the subject of the encomium. In Thucydides' *History* (2.35), Pericles is given the honour of delivering a funeral oration that is somewhat self-reflective on the Greek practice of giving and hearing such a speech. Pericles approaches the task of praising the fallen soldiers with some caution, because

> The hearer who is cognizant of the facts and partial to the dead will perhaps think that scant justice has been done in comparison with his own wishes and his own knowledge, while he who is not so informed, whenever he hears of an exploit which goes beyond his own capacity, will be led by envy to think there is some exaggeration. And indeed eulogies of other men are tolerable only in so far as each hearer thinks that he too has the ability to perform any of the exploits of which he hears; but whatever goes beyond that at once excites envy and unbelief.

Auditors of an epideictic speech that aimed at praise apparently responded, if the speech was successfully constructed, with a feeling of emulation, affirming themselves internally as they heard the speech with words like 'I could do that if I had to', and being drawn by the orator's praise into the conviction that one could oneself also act in a similarly praiseworthy manner. If one began to distance oneself from the subject of praise and from the possibility of upholding the values for which he or she was praised, the auditors would become unfavourable hearers.

The audience of *4 Maccabees* would have heard the speech not only as a philosophical demonstration but also as an encomium. The author signals this by introducing his speech as a 'praise' of rational judgment (1.2) and by proposing to 'praise for their virtues those who…died for the sake of nobility and goodness' (1.10). The audience would recognize that *4 Maccabees* shared many elements with encomia, particularly the civic funeral oration (the *epitaphios logos*). Education in rhetoric—even at the more elementary level (the *progymnasmata*)—included detailed instructions concerning the elements of encomia. Laudable elements were sought for in external excellences such as noble birth, the excellence of the subject's native city and ancestors, and 'personal advantages' such as education, reputation, public service, the number and beauty of one's children, and dying well. A second area in which praise was fitting was physical excellence, which included strength, beauty and capacity for deep feeling. 'Spiritual excellences' provided the third and most important element of an encomia. Under this heading the virtues exemplified by the subject (wisdom, temperance, courage, justice, piety, nobility and greatness of soul) would be discussed, together with the ways in which these virtues manifested themselves in service for the public good. The most praiseworthy actions were 'altruistic', 'good', rather than 'utilitarian or pleasant', 'in the public interest', and enacted while 'braving risks and dangers'. Common ways of enhancing the praiseworthiness of such actions were to emphasize how the subject performed them 'at great cost' to himself or herself, or achieved them 'alone' or 'with few to help' (criteria adapted from Marrou 1956: 272-73).

The reader of *4 Maccabees* will immediately observe that almost all of these elements have a counterpart in that oration. Eleazar's priestly lineage (which was considered 'noble birth' among the Jewish people, 5.4), the excellence of Jerusalem under the Torah-observant rule of Onias (3.20), the martyrs' common education in the Torah (5.4; 5.22-24, 34; 9.2; 18.10-18), the observations concerning the 'beauty and the

number' of the mother's children (8.3-5), the repeated sanctioning of
their deaths as noble or blessed (1.10; 10.15; 12.1), and the deep capacity for fraternal affection and parental love of the seven brothers and
their mother (13.19-27; 14.13-20; 15.6-11) all contribute to the 'exte-
rior' and 'bodily excellences' of the martyrs. More prominent is the
author's demonstration of the 'spiritual excellences' of these martyrs as
examples of each of the virtues listed above and as exemplars of dying
on behalf of virtue and of the whole nation. I shall look more closely at
this aspect of the encomium—the aspect which could be assimilated
and imitated by the audience—below.

4 Maccabees shares a number of other important features particularly
with the funeral oration (the *epitaphios logos*). Quintilian (*Institutes*
3.7.10-18) adds to the discussion of encomia in the *progymnasmata* the
observation that 'it would be creditable to the objects of our praise not
to have fallen short of the fair fame of their country and of their sires'.
J. W. van Henten (1995: 308) affirms that the the presentation of illustrious predecessors in 2.1–3.18 is similar to Athenian funeral speeches
which show that the deeds of the fallen are not isolated events but 'part
of a long, glorious tradition which showed the extraordinary character
of the citizens of Athens', or in the case of *4 Maccabees*, the Jewish
nation. This would also be true of 16.16-23, 18.11-13 and the numerous places where the author compares the martyrs' achievement with
the acts of a figure from the sacred history (e.g. the comparison of
Eleazar with Aaron in 7.11-12) in order to show how they do not fall
short of their ancestors, but rather preserve the honour of their race (cf.
5.18, 29; 6.17).

Moreover, the speech climaxes in 17.2-24 with an '*enumeratio* of the
glorious acts of all the martyrs' (van Henten 1993: 121), which is an
element of the Athenian funeral oration. This *enumeratio* contains a
proposal for an honourary inscription (a frequent literary device in
funeral orations and similar settings: cf. Lysias, *Orations* 2.1; Demosthenes, *Funeral Speech* 60.1; Euripides, *Trojan Women* 1188-91), an
extended athletic metaphor for the martyrs' struggle, the announce-
ment of the crown for the victors (also well attested in inscriptions),
and, in 17.19-22, the affirmation of their consecration by God and the
application to them of sacrificial language. Each element has been
shown to have parallels with honourary inscriptions (van Henten 1994:
58-59). The political character of their deaths, as conquerors of a tyrant
and liberators of their native land, adds strongly to the impression of
hearing a funeral oration for fallen defenders of the native land.

Pericles praises soldiers who died defending their city, showing at
length the blessedness of such a death, the nobility of the cause for
which they died, and the immortal fame that the soldiers acquired by
their moment of courage. Even within an encomium, however, Pericles fosters the hearers' feeling of emulation by direct exhortation and
application: 'We who remain behind may hope to be spared their fate,
but must resolve to keep the same daring spirit against the foe' (2.43);
'It is for you to try to be like them. Make up your minds that happiness
depends on being free, and freedom depends on being courageous'
(2.44). Similarly, the author of *4 Maccabees* aimed at inspiring the feeling of emulation among his auditors, and sought to lead them into the
resolve to 'keep the same daring spirit', drawing them in by the hope
of honour and praiseworthy remembrance and by their own sense of
honour.

The Martyrs as Exemplars of Virtue

One of the main goals of the encomiastic aspect of *4 Maccabees* is to
demonstrate that being a devout Jew is consistent with the recognized
virtues of the Graeco-Roman world, that Torah-observance enhances
rather than hinders virtuous and honourable living. If the dominant
culture fails to recognize this, it is a discredit to the Greek world and
not to the Jew, but the Jew must at least recognize the connection
between loyalty to the ancestral way of life and the perfection of virtue.
The martyrs are therefore presented as being guided by every virtue
towards the defence and maintenance of the Jewish way of life. What
prevents them from embracing the Greek way of life is not their folly
or baseness, but their hatred for the vices of cowardice, impiety and
injustice. Their deaths should be seen as deaths 'for the sake of virtue'
(1.8), so that the audience, too, may commit itself to endure any
degree of deprivation with the same noble resolution.

Nobility (Kalokagathia and Aretē)
The martyrs' concern for their own honour and the honour of their
race shows them to be noble, virtuous people who choose to act in
accordance with the 'good', not the 'utilitarian or pleasant'. This is
made apparent, for example, in the seven brothers' rejection of Antiochus's patronage and the pleasures of the Greek way of life for the
sake of acting justly and courageously (8.1–9.9). The author therefore
evaluated the character of the martyrs as honourable, and associated

them in various ways with *kalokagathia*, a word used in the Septuagint only in this book. According to Danker (1982: 319), who traces the use of this word in inscriptions honouring benefactors,

> to describe a person as *kalokagathos* (a perfect gentleman) or *kalēkagathē* (a noble woman) was one of the highest terms of praise in the Greek vocabulary. In some inscriptions the term *kalokagathos* appears as an alternate expression for *anér tēs aretēs* (man of arete) and other terms used to describe high achievers or benefactors.

The martyrs died 'for the sake of *kalokagathia*' (1.10), die 'equipped with *kalokagathia*', their deaths attesting to their character (11.22; 15.9), and lived with 'a common zeal for *kalokagathia* (13.25). This same virtue and virtuous description, however, is also made available to those of 'temperate mind', who give religious reason dominion over their passions, that is, who follow the Torah with the same commitment as did the martyrs (3.17-18).

The martyrs act out of a commitment to *aretē*, which means 'excellence' or 'virtue' as well as the reputation for being of such a character. The brothers endure torture and die 'for the sake of *aretē*' (1.8; 10.10; 11.2) which assures them also of receiving the 'prize of *aretē* (9.8); once again the emulation of this devotion to 'excellence' is held up to the auditors in the form of a rhetorical question: 'What person who… knows that it is blessed to endure any suffering for the sake of *aretē*, would not be able to overcome the emotions though godliness?' (7.21-22). The martyrs are therefore evaluated positively throughout the oration as 'noble' (*kalos* and *gennaios*; 6.10; 7.8; 8.3; 9.13; 10.3; 15.24, 20). The author hereby claimed for those staunchly committed to the Torah the highest titles of distinction that the Greek world could offer.

Piety
The martyrs are especially credited with the virtue of 'piety' (*eusebeia*). This is not properly one of the four cardinal virtues of Stoicism or Platonism, but often appears as a replacement for one of those virtues (cf. Philo, *Spec. Leg.* 4.147; Xenophon, *Memorabilia.* 4.6). It may be regarded as an aspect of justice, 'giving to each thing what it is entitled in proportion to its worth' (Cicero, *Rhetorica ad Herennium* 3.2.3) where what is due to Deity is considered. In Plato's *Gorgias* (507), in which temperance is the ruling virtue, 'piety' and 'justice' are presented as parallel virtues: the first leads the temperate person to do what is proper with regard to the gods, while the second leads him or her to

do what is proper to other people. Piety and dutifulness are closely related values, as one sees in the frequent use of the epithet *pius* to describe the hero of the *Aeneid*, who is dependable, faithful and dutiful with regard to the requirements of family, country and divinities. As such, it is a very important social virtue. The martyrs in *4 Maccabees* highly value this virtue, in that they suffer and die 'for the sake of piety' or 'religion', of which the hearers are reminded throughout the oration (5.31; 7.16; 9.29; 15.12; 16.13, 17, 19). Their choices are determined by their refusal to violate their life of piety and their reputation for this virtue (9.6, 25; 13.8, 10; 15.1, 3); as such, their deaths become a demonstration of piety (13.10). The way in which piety is linked with loyalty to God and the Torah (*pistis*) is especially important for the audience's own situation. They, like the martyrs, could fulfil the virtue of piety only by remaining loyal to their ancestral way of life.

Courage

The martyrs' endurance of brutal tortures is transformed from a fearful, degrading experience into a feat of 'noble bravery' (1.8), a display of endurance that results in the defeat of the tyrant, the liberation of their homeland, and the admiration even of their enemies (1.11; 17.23). The author thus interprets the martyrs' deaths in line with discussions of 'courage' in Greek ethics: Aristotle (*Nicomachean Ethics* 3.7.2 [1115b12]; cf. *Virt.* 4.4) defines courage as the endurance of fearful things 'for the sake of what is noble'; even the endurance of 'disgrace or pain' is praiseworthy, if it is suffered 'as the price of some great and noble object' (*Nicomachean Ethics* 3.1.7 [1110a20-22]). Their endurance of the most extreme tortures to the point of death for the sake of their honour and nation shows them to possess a virtue which was highly praised in Greek culture (frequently linked with military or athletic settings; cf. Pericles' funeral oration).

Eleazar specifically rejects the cowardly course, and the author weaves in a sort of philosophical inversion of the 'old head on young shoulders' *topos* (according to Theon, a possible element of encomium; Marrou 1956: 273). He chooses death, since he was 'not so old and cowardly as not to be young in reason on behalf of piety' (5.31). The author specifically draws attention to the endurance that he displayed as being beyond expectation for one so old: 'though he was an old man, his body no longer tense and firm, his muscles flabby, his sinews feeble, he became young again in spirit through reason' (7.13-14). That Eleazar endured pain and disgrace for the sake of keeping faith with his instructor (the Torah) and his ancestors shows his death to be a noble act of courage as Aristotle had defined it. The seven brothers are also specifically credited with acting courageously. The author's presentation of the course of action they did not choose, which he brands as cowardly (8.16), highlights the courageous spirit of their actual response to Antiochus, after which the brothers endured the tortures bravely (14.9).

The greatest example of courage, however, was the mother, the final and climactic subject of this 'narrative demonstration'. The author has expanded the brief notice given to the mother's admirable firmness in his source (2 Macc. 7.20) into a complete encomium for her endurance and commitment to virtue. In his lack of reticence in praising a woman, he departed from the opinion of Thucydides and follows rather the path of Plutarch in his 'On the Bravery [or, Virtue] of Women'. Thucydides closed Pericles' funeral oration with a few words about female virtue (*Histories* 2.45.2): 'great also is her [honour] of whom there is least talk among men whether in praise or in blame'. Plutarch, however, preferred 'the Roman custom, which publicly renders to women, as to men, a fitting commemoration after the end of their life' (*Moralia* 242F). Because 'man's virtues and woman's virtues are one and the same' (*Moralia* 243A), comparing the lives of virtuous men and women leads to a clarification of what virtue itself is (*Moralia* 243C).

The mother is credited with demonstrating endurance and courage—typically 'male' virtues in the ancient world (cf. 15.23)—more fully than any man (15.30). The mother is praised in terms familiar from the portrayal of courageous women in the Greek world. Here Plutarch's collection of these stories ('On the Bravery of Women') affords a convenient point of comparison with the encomium. Like the women of Chios (*Moralia* 245A), who urge the men to continue resistance against the enemy rather than agree to dishonourable surrender, the mother urges her sons to resist the tyrant even unto death rather than give up disgracefully (16.13). Like the women of Argos (*Moralia* 245D-E) who take up arms and repel the foreign invaders themselves, this woman also became a 'soldier of God' whose courage defeated the tyrant (16.14-15).

Perhaps no example among Plutarch's collection is so close to the mother of the seven as that of Megisto. The tyrant Aristotimus sought to undermine an attack from the exiled men of his city by inducing their wives, whom he imprisoned, to plead with their husbands through letters to abort their purpose.

> If they would not write, he threatened to put them all to death after torturing them and making away with their children first... Megisto, the wife of Timoleon,...made answer to him: 'I pray that they may never entertain so base a thought that, to spare their wives and little children, they should forsake the cause of their country's freedom...' Aristotimus...ordered her young child to be brought, as if intending to kill him in her sight. As the servants sought for him mingled among the other children playing and wrestling, his mother, calling him by name, said, 'Come here, child, and before you can realize and think, be delivered from this bitter despotism; since for me it is more grievous to look upon your undeserved slavery than your death' (*Moralia* 252A-C).

Megisto is very much like the mother in *4 Maccabees*, preferring death for her sons to ignoble submission to a tyrant, reinterpreting death in their situation as a blessing rather than an evil, and enduring (or being willing to endure) the sight of the child's death and not being weakened in her own resolve in order to spare the child's life. The mother, just as the male soldier, shows the quintessence of courage, namely, the willingness to endure what is fearful 'for the sake of what is noble' (Aristotle, *Nicomachean Ethics* 3.7.2 [1115b12]).

Self Control, Justice and Wisdom

The topic of the philosophical discourse, namely that 'devout reason is master of the emotions', leads naturally to the presentation of the martyrs as exemplars of self control. We have already seen in the preceding chapter how Eleazar masters pain, the brothers master pain, the prospect of pleasure and fraternal affection, and the mother masters love for offspring in order to persevere in virtue and live nobly. They are also presented, however, as examples of justice. Rhetoricians and ethicists considered justice to embrace a wide range of obligations:

> We shall be using the topics of Justice...if we show that it is proper to repay the well-deserving with gratitude...if we urge that faith (*fidem*) ought zealously to be kept...if we contend that alliances and friendships should scrupulously be honoured; if we make it clear that the duty imposed by nature towards parents, gods, and the fatherland (*in parentes, deos, patriam*) must be religiously observed; if we maintain that ties of hospitality, clientage, kinship, and relationship by marriage must inviolably be cherished; if we show that neither reward nor favour nor peril nor animosity ought to lead us astray from the right path (Cicero, *Rhetorica ad Herennium* 3.3.4; cf. also Aristotle, *Rhetorica ad Alexandrum* 1421b36-40).

Eleazar is thus demonstrating his commitment to justice when he refuses to 'transgress the sacred oaths of [his] ancestors' (5.29) or violate his ancestral law (5.33), playing false (breaking faith) with the Torah or the duties of a priest and elder (5.34). The brothers and their mother, moreover, act so as to maintain the ties of clientage with the God who granted them life and a 'share in the world' (13.13; 16.18-19). Neither the tyrant's promises of favour nor the peril of torture and death sway these brothers from 'the right path'. The brothers' submission to the counsel of their mother and their father (who speaks through the mother in (18.10-18), moreover, reinforces the impression of these young men as just, as they show the honour due to their parents in their actions. The author specifically mentions how the fraternal and maternal affection among the mother and her sons was heightened on account of the brothers' commitment to the virtue of justice (13.24; 15.10).

Finally, the martyrs display the virtue of wisdom, which includes the correct weighing of advantages and disadvantages and discernment of the correct course through judicious analysis of precedents (examples from the past; cf. Cicero, *Rhetorica ad Herennium* 3.3.4). The brothers weigh the prospects of temporary advantage from accepting Antiochus's offer of patronage against the eternal disadvantage of breaking faith with God and thus incurring judgment (13.14-16); the mother similarly weighs the temporary safety of her children, should she persuade them to eat the pork, against their eternal safety with God, should she urge them on to die loyal to the Torah, casting her ballot in favour of the latter (15.2-3, 8, 25-28). The many examples of past faithfulness used by the brothers and the mother to encourage one another also represent the virtue of wisdom in action, leading them to discern what is truly the advantageous and right course of action.

The martyrs' choice, then, to die for the Torah rather than accept assimilation into the dominant culture represents a choice in which all the virtues prized by that dominant culture are combined. The hearers of the oration are made to consider, therefore, that the path of virtue, and hence the honourable course of action, is to remain themselves loyal to the Jewish way of life. By such means, they, too, may be remembered by future generations as exemplars of virtue who, exercised by and committed to the Torah, attained the full measure of nobility.

Transforming Disgrace into Honourable Victory

There is a striking tension between the author's assessment of the martyr as the paragon of virtue and the evaluation and treatment of the
martyr by the representatives of the dominant Greek culture whose
virtues they are supposed to fulfil and perfect. Honour or dishonour
were often represented physically in the ancient world: bowing to a
person symbolized the recognition of his or her honour; physical abuse
reflected the lack of honour ascribed by those doing the mistreating
(see Malina and Neyrey 1991). The martyr's worth was symbolically
degraded as the torturers assaulted his physical body.

The author, conscious of this, makes it clear that the physical treatment endured by Eleazar, for example, in no way detracted from his
true honour. The tyrant's henchmen might strip him (part of the sta-
tus-degradation ritual), but he remained 'adorned with the gracefulness
of his piety' (6.2); they might beat him until his physical body collapses
to the ground, but 'he kept his reason upright and unswerving' (6.7).
What was decisive for honour was the maintenance of the 'upright reason' (*orthos logos*; cf. 1.15) which chooses the path of virtue rather than
giving in to the demands of the passions. As in Plato's *Gorgias* (523D-
525A), it was the state of the soul, not the state of the body, that mat-
tered for the verdict of the eternal court: the graceful trappings of the
body may hide a soul scarred by vice. Thus Eleazar, though disgraced
in life, enjoys the honour of a noble soul, decorated by all the virtues,
and the assurance of the favourable reception that he will receive from
his Judge; conversely, the audience will be made aware of the torments
that will await Antiochus IV, even though he sits in state now, because
of his wickedness and vice (9.8-9; 10.10-11; 12.11-14).

The audience needed to understand how their lack of honour and
ignorance of virtue in the sight of most members of the dominant culture was in fact no reflection on their true honour or nobility. Further-
more, they needed to be assured that any endurance of apparent disgrace
(such as insult or physical abuse) was not in reality a blow against their
honour. To accomplish this, the author interprets the martyrs' experience of disgrace and abuse in terms of philosophical discussions of the
ideal sage, the disgrace of the one who persecutes the virtuous, the
metaphor of the athletic competition, and the noble death.

The Martyrs as Exemplars of the Philosophers' Ideal Sage
Freedom from slavery to the passions is a primary goal of the philosopher, and, as we have seen in Chapter 3, the author stresses primarily

this freedom as the fruit of a life committed to the Torah. Physical slavery was considered to be a disgraceful state; it was far more disgraceful, according to the philosophers, to be slaves inwardly to one's own passions and tendencies toward vice (cf. Philo, *Omn. Prob. Lib.* 17). Freedom, the peace of the mind that is able to check the authority of the passions, was a noble ideal.

The author praises the martyrs' mastery of the emotions using a number of maritime metaphors familiar to Hellenistic philosophy, Greek drama and Hellenistic Jewish writings. First, Eleazar's reasoning faculty is likened to a pilot steering the 'ship of religion over the sea of the emotions [passions]' (7.1). Despite the fierce onslaught of the winds of the tyrant's threats and the waves of the tortures, it kept the 'rudder of religion' straight (like the *orthos logos*) until the safe harbour of unassailable virtue was reached, namely the undiscovered country beyond death (7.2-3). This image is often used of a political king (Sophocles, *Oed. Tyr.* 689-696; *Ant.* 994-95); there are even more numerous parallels of the metaphor being applied to 'reason' as the pilot that steers, or should steer, the whole creature (Euripides, *Trojan Women* 686-96; Philo, *Leg. All.* 3.118, 223-24). Eleazar's mind was set as 'a jutting cliff' which the surf can pound but not move—the waves of the passions broke over its hardness (7.5; cf. Seneca, *De constantia* 3.5).

Similarly, the seven brothers, who were not 'slaves to their emotions' (13.2), are likened to a fortified harbour bearing the onslaught of the waves of the ocean of passions, making a safe haven for their virtue (13.6-7). Finally, the image used to portray the mother's trial and victory is that of Noah's ark, 'carrying the world in the universal flood' (15.31) So the mother's reason 'endured the waves' of the emotions and passions, preserving the religion of the nation. Philo (*Quaest. in Gen.* 2.18) had also used the story of Noah's ark as an allegory of the soul's struggle for virtue:

> And this is truly a great flood when the streams of the mind are opened by folly, madness, insatiable desire, wrongdoing, senselessness, recklessness, and impiety; and when the fountains of the body are opened by sensual pleasure, desire, drunkenness, gourmandism, and licentiousness with kin and sisters and by incurable vices.

This is a particularly Jewish recasting, though not reshaping, of the more general image of the ship steering across a troubled sea, encountered in 7.1-3.

A second important element in the presentation of the martyrs as ideal sages was freedom from external compulsion—the application of external force in the attempt to dominate the mind (cf. 5.16; 6.9; 8.1, 14, 22, 24; 9.6). Such freedom was an ideal for which ancient philosophers earnestly strove and which they held before their pupils as the goal of philosophy. Epictetus held this ideal especially dear: 'the man over whom pleasure has no power, nor evil, nor fame, nor wealth, and who, whenever it seems good to him, can spit his whole paltry body into some oppressor's face and depart from this life—whose slave can he any longer be, whose subject?' (*Discourses* 3.24.71; 4.1.60, 87; cf. Philo, *Omn. Prob. Lib.* 30). Aristotle (*Nicomachean Ethics* 3.1.9 [1110a32-33]) further noted that, with regard to actions to which one ought never to consent, even under compulsion, 'praise and blame are bestowed according as we do or do not yield to such compulsion'.

The portrayal of Antiochus as the tyrant facilitated the portrayal of the martyrs as the philosophers' 'wise person', who endured every torment rather than give up their freedom and yield to external compulsions. They were such 'masters of themselves' that the tyrant's weapons—both tortures (5.27-28; 9.17) and promises of favour (9.4)—were powerless to achieve his goal of dominating them (5.38; cf. Cicero, *Tusculun Disputations* 2.22.52-54; Epictetus, *Discourses* 4.1). Notable here is the importance of the Torah as the trainer that enables the Jew to withstand and defeat the compulsion of the tyrant, where the 'impious', whose minds have not been trained by the constant exercise of Torah-observance, might succumb (5.38; cf. Philo, *Omn. Prob. Lib.* 60, 97; Cicero, *Paradoxa Stoicorum* 5.1.34; Epictetus, *Discourses* 1.12.9). By such standards, Eleazar and the other martyrs showed themselves to be most honourable people as they successfully withstood the attempts at compulsion. They realized the achievement of the 'wise person' who would 'do nothing of which he can repent, nothing against his will', but would 'do everything nobly, consistently, soberly, rightly' (Cicero, *Tusculun Disputations* 5.81).

A third topic familar from philosophical texts is the wise person's freedom from injury. A distinction between power over life and power over injury is familiar to Hellenistic ethical philosophy. Socrates was well known for his statement of his opponents' limited power: 'Anytus and Meletus can kill me, but they cannot injure me' (Epictetus, *Manual* 53.4; cf. Plato, *Apology* 18 [30C-D]). For Socrates, the only injury which could befall him was a lapse of virtue, which would indeed harm his soul. Seneca concurred with this definition of injury, and so his 'wise man can receive neither injury or insult'; 'the wise man is safe, and no injury or insult can touch him' (*De constantia* 2.1, 3). So also the author attributed to the brothers this highly philosophical and respectable concept: 'if you take our lives because of our religion, do not suppose that you can injure us by torturing us' (9.7). For them, capitulation would be injury, for that would entail the loss of virtue and the reward that it brings at God's hands. Death at the tyrant's hands, however, does not inflict any lasting harm.

The Persecutor's Disgrace

The author spends no little effort insulating his audience from the negative opinion of the non-Jew. For adherents of a subculture like Judaism in the midst of a rarely appreciative dominant culture, it was essential that members of the subculture regard the Gentile's negative opinion of them as a negative reflection on the Gentile. This, too was a familiar topic of philosophical discourse, as philosophers regularly point out that only the opinion of the wise person, or the one who knows and cares about virtue, is worth considering, while the opinion of the masses—whether a favourable or unfavourable opinion—is worthless (Plato, *Crito* 46C-47D; Seneca, *De constantia* 13.2, 5; 19.3).

When Antiochus, therefore, evaluated Eleazar's noble choice as 'madness' (*mania*, 8.5), this opinion does Eleazar's reputation no serious harm since the author has already demonstrated that Eleazar lived and died in the practice of every virtue, and so died nobly. Antiochus's judgment of Eleazar would have been heard rather as, in effect, Antiochus's own failure to recognize virtue, a fruit of his own baseness. Epictetus (*Discourses* 1.29.50-54) describes how such judgments reveal more about the judge than the judged. If a governor judges the philosopher to be impious and profane, this judgment has no more value than a judgment he might make about some hypothetical syllogism, declaring,

> 'I judge the statement, "If it is day, there is light", to be false'. Who is being judged in this case, who has been condemned? The hypothetical syllogism, or the man who has been deceived in his judgement about it? Who in the world, then, is the man who has authority to make any declaration about you? Does he know what piety or impiety is? Has he pondered the matter? Has he learned it? Shall the truly educated man pay attention to an uninstructed person when he passes judgement on what is holy and unholy, and on what is just and unjust?

Moreover, suffering punishment or abuse at the hands of Gentiles on account of being a Jew is a sign not of the Jew's dishonour, but rather of the dishonour of the Gentile perpetrators. The eldest brother, for

example, charges the tyrant with acting unjustly: 'Most abominable
tyrant, enemy of heavenly justice, savage of mind, you are mangling
me in this manner, not because I am a murderer, or as one who acts
impiously, but because I protect the divine law' (9.15). He knew that
he was suffering unjustly, and that the physical punishments reflected
not his own criminal behaviour but rather the tyrant's viciousness. This
recalls the fundamental issue in Plato's *Gorgias*, namely, whether it is
worse to suffer unjustly or to act unjustly, Socrates arguing cogently
that the one who does the injustice, though physically unscathed, is
much worse off in the long run since injustice mars the soul and
endangers one's eternal well-being. The young man receives no dishonour from the physical assaults: 'he who does the injustice is the one
to blush' (Seneca, *De constantia* 16.4). The author continues to resonate
with Plato's *Gorgias*, specifically with Socrates' argument that virtue
alone is the cause of happiness, while vice alone brings wretchedness
(470E-471A; cf. Plutarch, *Can Vice Cause Unhappiness* 2 [*Moralia* 498C-
E]; Cicero, *Tusculun Disputations* 5.51-67). According to Socrates, 'the
temperate man…being just and brave and pious, is the perfection of a
good man; and…the good man does well and fairly whatever he does;
and … he who does well is blessed and happy, while the wicked man
or evil-doer is wretched' (*Gorgias* 507B-C; cf. Cicero, *Tusculun Disputations* 5.73-82). Here in *4 Maccabees*, the pain is lightened by the joy
that virtue brings, namely the knowledge that one remains true to God
and will partake of the eternal joy that God prepares for the pious;
Antiochus is indeed 'wretched' because of his injustice, but will come
to know fiercer pain through divine vengeance (9.30-31). His vice is
here thought already to carry the threat and pain of its own impending
punishment.

The author places upon the lips of the martyrs several extended criticisms of Antiochus and, indirectly in his person, of those Gentiles who
are hostile toward the Jewish people. The fifth brother accuses Antiochus of not understanding what acts are virtuous and worthy of honour and which are vicious and worthy of punishment. He is ignorant in
those matters in which it is most contemptible not to have knowledge
(cf. Plato, *Gorgias* 472C). Again, the echoes of Socrates' verdict that it
is more shameful to act unjustly than to suffer injustice are heard (cf.
Gorgias 508C-E; Epictetus, *Discourses* 4.1.123; Seneca, *De constantia*
16.4). Here, however, something more is added. Antiochus, and with
him the portion of the Gentile world that despises or seeks to harm the
Jewish people on account of their exclusive devotion to the One God

and strict observance of God's Torah (11.5), cannot make a proper evaluation of what is honourable or censurable. Such persons act out of an ignorance of what is truly virtuous, and so their opinions are false and cannot be allowed to sway loyal Jews away from their commitment. Their anti-Jewish actions, based on those errant opinions that the Torah promotes 'hatred of strangers' and 'atheism', are not to deter loyal Jews from practising their religion, for they are based not on any accurate knowledge of virtue or its opposite. Indeed, anti-Jewish actions may thus come to promote Jewish commitment, for it becomes a sign of the darkness and error that descends upon human minds that are unenlightened by God. Rather than give in to the social pressure, the Diaspora Jew may take up the fifth brother's censure: 'these deeds deserve honours, not tortures!'

Finally, the seventh brother censures the persecutor for failing to show gratitude to God and to act humanely toward fellow human beings (12.11-14). The Gentile, like the Jew, receives all good things from God: how, therefore, could the Gentiles be so shameless as to fail to honour this God and, to add injury to insult, abuse God's loyal clients (12.11-12)? Moreover, how can Gentiles be so shameless as to violate that common bond of humanity by abusing people 'who have feelings like [theirs] and are made of the same elements as [them]' (12.13-14; cf. Epictetus, *Discourses* 1.13.3-5)? The notion of the oneness of human nature, transcending social, ethnic and civic status, became quite popular in the Hellenistic period and into the Roman period (cf. Wis. 7.1-3; Heb. 2.11; Acts 14.15; Jas 5.9; Ignatius, *Trall.* 10). Again, a criticism levelled against the Jews (for their divisiveness, their refusal to mix with or show kindness to those of other races) is turned back upon the Gentile, who in rejecting, ridiculing, or abusing the loyal Jew violates the same principle of humanity's essential commonality.

The brothers' warning to the tyrant that eternal judgment and punishment awaited him, a theme running throughout their encounter (9.32b; 10.11, 21; 11.3; 12.11-14), was also a common theme in philosophical writings (cf. Seneca, *Hercules Furens* 731-46; Lucian, *Tyrant* 25-28). The loyal Jew could therefore be assured that any injustice perpetrated upon his or her person in this life would be avenged in the next, vindicating his or her honour. The audience, moreover, would be doubly strengthened by the author's connection of commitment to the Torah with the perfection of virtue and this demonstration of the error of Gentiles in their assessment of Jews. They would be emboldened to endure hostility, knowing that it was no mark against their honour or self respect.

Athletic Imagery

The imagery of the athletic competition, usually images drawn from boxing or wrestling, runs throughout *4 Maccabees* (6.10; 9.8, 23; 11.20-23; 12.11, 14; 13.13, 15; 16.16; 17.11-16). Athletic imagery was a useful way to turn the hardships often encountered by the devotee of philosophy (insult, scorn, poverty, loss of reputation, even physical abuse and execution) from experiences of disgrace into a quest for honour in the eyes of the wise as well as for self respect. The image affords many similarities: athletes submitted to harsh trainers, disregarded the views of the many in favour of whatever the trainer thought best, endured pain in the ring and jeers from the crowd, all in order to attain honour through victory. Dio Chrysostom (*Orations* 8.18), for example, compares the philosopher who wrestles with hardships, the most 'difficult of antagonists', with an athlete. The philosopher, however, competes for a superior, hence more noble, prize—not for a mere sprig of a tree (the victor's wreath) or for the transitory prizes of people's acclaim or awards of money, but for the prize of virtue. Epictetus graced the life of the Stoic and the Cynic philosopher with the label of 'Olympic contests' (*Discourses* 3.22.56), and exalted the hardships suffered by the true philosopher as divine training (*Discourses* 3.22.56; 1.24.1), by which God fitted one to be an 'invincible athlete' (*Discourses* 1.18.21) or 'Olympic victor' (*Discourses* 1.24.2). By such means, a way of life that often met with ridicule from the members of the majority culture was given a new honour and nobility (and hence motivation) for those open to philosophy.

Eleazar, enduring a severe flagellation, is likened to 'a noble athlete' who is victorious over his antagonists, the torturers, because he can endure as much or more than they can inflict (6.9-10). Similarly, the sixth brother, who interprets the torments as a 'contest befitting holiness' (11.20), proclaims that he and his brothers have gone undefeated (11.20b), for they have not succumbed to the blows of the tyrant. This is another familiar image from Stoic ethical philosophy. Philo, for example, compares the 'virtuous man' with a boxer who conquers by letting an opponent wear himself out by beating against his hardened flesh (*Omn. Prob. Lib.* 26-27; cf. Seneca, *De constantia* 9.4). Such unconquered reason (11.27), which could withstand the onslaught of the passions yet not give in to a base impulse, was the noble goal of the popular philosophers (cf. Seneca, *Epistulae Morales* 67.16; cf. *De constantia* 5.6-7).

In his closing celebration of the martyrs, the author develops this image most completely (17.11-16). Here, the engagement with the

Gentile world over the survival of Judaism as a way of life is a 'divine'
contest: the attempts of Antiochus to entice through promises or compel through violence are resisted by the 'athletes' of piety, and their
endurance opens the way for them not to death and disgrace, but to
'immortality in endless life' (17.12). Just as the martyrs were aware of
the public nature of their trial, and sought to preserve the honour of
God and the nation before this arena, so the author here acknowledges
the 'spectators' of the contest—'the world and the human race'—who
witnessed their victory (17.14). The life of the philosopher as a 'spectacle' before God and humanity appears frequently in Stoic literature
(Seneca, *De providentia* 2.9; Epictetus, *Discourses* 3.22.58-59), and the
philosopher remains always a witness to the truth of what his or her
philosophy promises (cf. Epictetus's 'witness' in *Discourses* 1.29.44-49).

So in *4 Maccabees*, the martyrs bore a faithful witness with their lives
to the claims made by the author (in his own voice and in Eleazar's
voice) that the Torah inculcated fully and perfectly the cardinal virtues.
Their actions showed to the world that Jews were the match of anyone
in endurance, courage and piety, and that no promise or pain could
turn them aside from virtue. This is the same 'noble contest' for which
the mother encouraged her children—not only the seven brothers, but
the whole Jewish people, including the author's audience. They, too,
bear witness before the arena of spectators, and may attain the crown
which virtue bestows and 'stand in honour before God' along with the
martyrs (17.5) if they bear faithful witness and compete nobly.

Beneficial Death
The final means by which the author transforms a disgraceful death into
a noble end involves the interpretation of their deaths as 'happy' or
'blessed' (1.10; 7.22; 10.15; 12.1; *euthanasia*, 'dying well', was an important element of the encomium). The death of the martyrs, far from
being a fearsome thing to be avoided, is praised as 'blessed' or 'enviable'
by the author (1.10) on account of the honour that they win. Such a
claim would be familiar from classical funeral orations. Lysias (*Orations*
2.81), for example, thus praises the fallen soldiers: 'I, indeed, call them
blessed in their death, and envy them; I hold that for those alone
amongst men is it better to be born who, having received mortal bodies,
have left behind an immortal memory arising from their valour'.

The author affirms their deaths as noble since incurred 'for the sake
of virtue' (1.8) and piety (6.22; 7.16, 22; 9.6, 7, 30; 11.20; 16.17;
17.7). Their deaths were the proof and capstone of the martyrs' virtue.

It was precisely when their virtue was put to the test that their lives could be seen as exemplary and praiseworthy: the end of their lives colours the portrayal of the whole as dedicated to piety, courage and the other virtues. It is in the outcome of their lives that their honour is secured, even as Pericles looks to the soldiers' deaths as the seal of their virtue (Thucydides, *Histories* 2.42). As the consummation of piety and courage, therefore, the martyrs' suffering and dying is lauded as done 'nobly' or 'blessedly' (6.30; 9.24; 10.1, 15; 11.12; 12.1, 14; 15.32; 16.16).

The author calls Eleazar's death a 'faithful seal' that 'perfected' Eleazar's life (7.15). This is somewhat related to the sober saying that concludes Sophocles' *Oedipus Tyrannus*, to the effect that no mortal should be called happy until he or she is dead and beyond the reach of pain. Just as tragedy may turn joy into sorrow in a single day, so some weakness of character may ruin a virtuous life in a single day. Eleazar knew that his reputation for piety demonstrated through a long life of devotion was in jeopardy in the contest with Antiochus. He would become immediately a 'pattern of impiety' in one instant if he failed to remain firm (5.18, 6.19). Eleazar's virtue was not complete until it could no longer be threatened, no longer be assailed. Death removed him from the possibility of ever polluting himself. By dying honourably, the honour of his life would forever remain intact (cf. Epictetus, *Discourses* 3.20.4-6). In this sense, Eleazar's death was a blessed one, even though one preceded by the greatest pains.

The mother's death—even death by suicide—was also interpreted as the preservation of virtue. She threw herself into the flames of the brazier 'so that no one might touch her body' (17.1), choosing suicide as a noble way to avoid disgrace or outrage (compare Saul's rationale for suicide in 1 Sam. 31.1-6; also Razis in 2 Macc. 14.41-46; Josephus, *War* 7.324-334, 377). In her death, the mother preserves her chastity, a virtue that is developed in the mother's second speech (18.6-19) and which balances display of 'courage' (*andreia*), a virtue whose very etymology points to its 'male' quality (15.5–16.14). Both Greeks and Jews agreed that women achieved their virtue by remaining in the private spaces of the home, and lost it by straying out from under a father's or husband's roof. Thus Euripides (*Trojan Women* 645-53) frames Andromache's boast: 'this very thing shall bring ill fame, if [a woman] abide not in the home: so banished I such craving, kept the house'. Philo (*Spec. Leg.* 3.169) is in complete agreement: 'women are best suited to the indoor life which never strays from the house, within which the middle door is taken by the maidens as their boundary, and the outer door by those who have reached full womanhood'. So also the mother, despite her brave and praiseworthy performance in the public arena of Antiochus, prizes also her domestic virtue and the preservation of her chastity (18.7-9a). Interesting here is the threat to female virginity posed not only by men but also by 'the deceitful serpent', perhaps indicative also of a sexual reading of the Fall narrative in Genesis 3 current in the author's circles.

The martyrs were not only honoured for their moral achievement as individuals, holding fast to piety even unto death, for which they have received eternal reward at God's hands (17.18-20a), but also for becoming the benefactors of their nation in two distinct but related ways. First, their steadfast obedience became the means by which God was reconciled to his people, and his favour toward them was once again secured (see discussion of 'Atonement' in Chapter 6 below). Secondly, by their unflagging resistance, they drove Antiochus from the land of Israel and liberated their compatriots from tyranny (17.20; 18.4-5). Liberation from tyranny was regarded as an especially valuable benefit (cf. Lucian, *Tyrannicide* 4, 7), and the vocabulary of the 'epitaph' of 17.9-10 is especially similar to pagan sources on a tyrant's abolition of a democracy as well as to the celebration of those who liberate a city or state from tyranny or other threat (van Henten 1994: 64-65). Their deaths are thus rendered noble and praiseworthy on account of the benefit they brought to others by dying (cf. Cicero, *Rhetorica ad Herennium* 3.7.14; Quintilian, *Institutes* 3.7.10-18). As the cause of noble ends, namely peace with God and freedom from tyranny, their deaths become things 'honourable and divine' (Aristotle, *Nicomachean Ethics* 1.12.7 [1102a2-4]). The author of *4 Maccabees* shows that 'the Jews had their own glorious heroes who could measure up to the pagan liberators from tyranny or other illustrious persons who sacrificed their lives for their people' (van Henten 1994: 69).

Townshend (1913: 684) and S.K. Williams (1975: 171) wish to read into 18.4-5 a brief reference to the exploits of the military heroes of the struggle against Antiochus IV, namely the Hamsonaean family. While it is historically true that the Hasmonaean family was responsible for restoring the Law and winning Jewish independence, the lack of a clear reference to any referent besides the martyrs in these verses (not to mention the grammatical acrobatics to which Williams must resort to give the Hasmonaeans a foothold in the verse) demonstrates that the author does not allow anyone to share the glory with the martyrs,

whose endurance and loyalty alone win the day. He ascribes to Eleazar
and the other martyrs the restoration of Torah-observance through
their example of holding fast to the dictates of the Torah.

This is all the more appropriate for a Diaspora setting, where fidelity
to the Law, not armed revolt, is the course of action to be honoured
and urged. Especially noteworthy in this regard is the connection
between Eleazar's motive in refusing even to pretend to eat pork (6.17-
19)—taking care not to set an example that might promote impiety
among his fellow Jews (6.19)—and the nation's eventual victory over
Antiochus (18.5). Eleazar's noble example of holding firm to the Torah
enables the seven brothers (9.5-7) and eventually the whole nation to
resist successfully the attempt to extend Greek cultural imperialism over
the Jewish people. Eleazar becomes a model held up explicitly for the
emulation of those entrusted with administering the community of the
faithful: 'such should be those who are administrators of the law,
shielding it with their own blood and noble sweat in sufferings even to
death' (7.8). This was a direct appeal to the leaders of the Diaspora
Jewish communities to attend not to advancing the standing of the
community through compromise with the dominant culture, but rather
to work to ensure the community's commitment to the Torah through
their own example. The examples further instructed each hearer concerning his or her responsibility to help others remain steadfast by setting a noble example.

Conclusion

The encomium for the martyrs would have led the hearers to understand that adherence to the Torah was in keeping with the life of
virtue—indeed that it led to the perfection of the virtues acknowledged
by Jew and Gentile alike. That Antiochus failed to recognize the virtue
of these martyrs showed his own dishonour and ignorance of noble
things, an observation that would also have helped insulate the audience from the effects of Gentile criticism, insult and hostility. The path
to honour remained, then, the path of the martyrs: commitment to the
Torah to the end resulted in a noble end to a noble life, lived in the
service of God and of the Jewish community. Thus, in the words of
van Henten (1994: 69), 'the triumphant martyrs show in an exemplary
way that faithfulness to the Lord and His law should be seen as the
basic principle of the life of the Jews'. Those who seek to answer the
demands of pagan society through loosening of observation of the
Torah act dishonourably and irreverently (e.g. Simon and Jason, 4.1-

21), gaining a shameful reputation, in the author's estimation of hon-
our, and earning the wrath of the Deity whom they despised through
disregarding the Law. The Torah-observant Jew, however, who
endures the noble contest for piety in the face of the threats and enticements of the Gentile world, will 'stand in honour before God' (17.5)
with the martyrs.

Further Reading

On Encomia and Commemorative Addresses
Quintilian (*Institutio Oratoria* 3.7.10-18) provides a brief prescription for the
composition of an encomium, and Marrou (1956: 272-73) offers a helpful
digest in outline form of Theon's discussion of the contents of encomia.
Lebram (1974) and van Henten (1994) contain perhaps the best discussions of
the similarities between *4 Maccabees* and the Athenian funeral oration.

The Contest Motif
A seminal discussion of the use of athletic imagery in Greco-Roman literature
appears in Pfitzner (1967: 23-48). deSilva (1995a) provides numerous examples
of the use of athletic imagery among philosophers, Jewish texts, and the Letter
to the Hebrews as a means of giving honour to supporting the values of subcul-
tures and countercultures.

The Martyrs and Atonement Language
The author's presentation of the martyrs' deaths as an atoning sacrifice that
benefits the whole nation by restoring God's favour is an important part of his
portrayal of their deaths as noble. This aspect of his interpretation of the martyrdoms will be discussed more fully in the section on 'Atonement' in Chapter
6 below. Important secondary literature includes O'Hagan (1974: 102-19);
Seeley (1990: 84-98); S. K. Williams (1975: 169-96). See also the literature at
the end of Chapter 6.

The Martyrs as Paradigms of Virtue
O'Hagan (1974: 99-102) and S. K. Williams (1975: 168-69) emphasize the
importance of the martyrs as exemplary figures who provide a pattern for virtuous living.

Suicide in the Ancient World
Suicide has come to be regarded as an ignoble act or even a mortal sin, but
ancient views on the subject differed dramatically from these modern views.
Droge and Tabor (1992) provide an important resource for positive assessments
of suicide in the Graeco-Roman and early Christian periods.

Quotations from Aristotle, Plutarch, Quintilian, Thucydides, the *Rhetorica ad Herennium*, Epictetus, Seneca, Cicero, Plato, Lysias and Euripides have been taken from the LCL editions; quotations from Philo, *Quod omnis probum liber sit*, have been taken from the LCL edition; all other quotations from Philo have been taken from the revised edition of Yonge's translation.

5

4 MACCABEES AS
PROTREPTIC DISCOURSE

The 'protreptic' element of *4 Maccabees* is not a third species alongside
the philosophical and encomiastic aspects of the text, but is rather the
guiding element that brings the philosophical, laudatory and deliberative elements together to renew or win commitment among the hearers to the Jewish way of life. The speech begins with an invitation to
'pay earnest attention to philosophy' (1.1), and the philosophical argument of the whole work will in itself be an important aspect of achieving the author's objective. His successful effort to show how
Torah-observance enables the individual to master the passions that
hinder virtue, and thus how Torah-observance leads the individual to
achieve the highest goal of Greek ethical philosophy, is the backbone
of his attempt to strengthen the hearers' loyalty to the Jewish way of
life. Throughout this demonstration, moreover, he makes ever more
exclusive claims for Torah-observance as the path to virtue and the
honourable state of mastering one's emotions. Victory over the emotions that hinder the practice of justice comes 'as soon as one adopts a
way of life in accordance with the law' (2.8). Similarly, in unfolding
God's provisions in the creation of humanity for a life of virtue, the
author states that 'to the mind he gave the Law; and one who lives
subject to this will rule a kingdom that is temperate, just, good and
courageous' (2.23). He asserts that 'as many as attend to religion with a
whole heart, these *alone* are able to control the passions of the flesh'
(7.18). Finally, the author has placed upon the lips of the eldest brother
the thesis that their deaths will demonstrate: 'I will convince you that
children of the Hebrews alone are invincible where virtue is concerned' (9.18). The hearers will be led by his demonstration of the
promise of this philosophy (namely, complete obedience to the Torah,
18.1) to see their own Jewish heritage as a priceless possession even in

terms that the dominant Greek culture should understand.

The author has gained a number of advantages by also embedding his protreptic discourse within an epideictic framework. While he could have chosen to write a more direct speech extolling the benefits of following the Torah and cautioning against the disadvantages of transgressing the Torah, by selecting an indirect approach he is able to guide the hearers' evaluation of the way of life he proposes. The choices that the martyrs make are demonstrated to be the choices that lead to honour and eternal advantage by the speech itself, which praises these figures and holds them up for the emulation of later generations. The endurance of the martyrs also demonstrates the value and credibility of the Jewish way of life (cf. *4 Macc.* 7.9). By witnessing their contest, their process of weighing alternatives, and their decision to remain steadfast, the audience will better appreciate the value of their way of life by the cost which the martyrs were willing to pay in order to preserve it. Moreover, the author has been able to appeal to the audience's emulation: by praising the martyrs as noble, virtuous and honoured in God's court, the author makes their choice to preserve their way of life highly desirable for the audience, as the hearers will hope for the same honour for themselves. Further, they might be shamed by the example of the martyrs for not valuing their way of life sufficiently, or for being unwilling to contend as bravely as they did for the Torah. The praise of the martyrs and their choices will embolden them to acquit themselves, as it were, with renewed boldness in preserving and defending the Jewish way of life.

We have also observed, however, that the author has reinforced the strengths of the philosophical discourse and the encomium by creating a deliberative environment within the speech that would invite the hearers also to deliberate within themselves concerning the commitments they would make. The audience is invited into the arena where the representative of Gentile power has confronted the representatives of the Jewish minority culture. They are allowed to hear in the mouth of Antiochus the same enticements and criticisms that they might daily face, and learn from the deliberations of the martyrs how fidelity to God and the Torah is indeed the only honourable and advantageous choice. It is to this element that I turn now.

Answering Objections to the Jewish Way of Life

J.W. van Henten (1995: 306-307) describes a pattern common to a number of Jewish martyr stories (Dan. 3, 6; 2 Macc 6.18-31; 7;

4 Macc.; Rabbinic texts such as *b. Ber.* 61b [Rabbi Akiba], *b. 'Abod. Zar.* 17b-18a [Rabbi Hanina ben Teradion]) in which, following the refusal of Jews to obey a recently promulgated Gentile decree that makes it impossible for Jews to stay faithful to their God or their Law, there is an episode of examination (sometimes under torture) in which the faithful Jew makes clear his or her resolution to die rather than obey the authorities. This element is usually the most prominent, and affords the author the opportunity to speak most directly to the audience about the reasons for remaining loyal to the ancestral way of life. In *4 Maccabees*, one finds two such episodes—Antiochus's conversation with Eleazar in ch. 5 and Antiochus's appeal to the seven brothers in ch. 8.

Klauck (1989a: 652) has fittingly called these *Rededuelle*, 'speech duels'. Antiochus, representing the voice of the dominant culture, takes his 'best shot' at the martyrs with philosophical considerations, threats and promises, and the martyrs return the fire with nobler philosophy, challenges to the tyrant, and assurances of divine vindication. Antiochus's speech in ch. 5 gives expression to some of the basic objections to the Jewish 'philosophy' that one finds in the dominant culture, as well as the primarily negative evaluation of Judaism. Eleazar's reply, however, wins for Judaism the status of a reasonable 'philosophy'. Even though this status is not acknowledged by Antiochus, the audience of *4 Maccabees* will be emboldened by Eleazar's eloquent defence and inspired by his heroic death 'for the sake of piety'.

The Character of Antiochus
Aristotle (*Rhetoric* 1.2.3-6) observed that the success of any speech rests not only upon the marshalling of rational arguments and the rousing of appropriate emotions in the audience, but also in the demonstration of the speaker's character and reliability. This is called *ēthos*—that which gives a speaker credibility and gives his words authority. In the world of speeches that the author of *4 Maccabees* has created in chs. 5–18, the addressees would consider not only the speech itself, but also the character of the speaker. How does the author present the 'orator' in the 'speech duels'? How does this presentation give weight to their opinions and arguments, or detract from their credibility?

Antiochus was first introduced as an 'arrogant and terrible man' (4.15), that is, one who failed to respect the boundaries between the human and the divine, treating his fellow human beings with shameless violence (12.13) and attacking laws reputed to be divine 'with a high hand'. Here he is presented as a 'tyrant' (5.1), a term carrying as much

$4^{15} + 5^1$ as undermining A4's ethos from the beginning.

ethical as political weight. Heininger (1989: 50-53) has helpfully shown that, while the figure of Eleazar was taken over from his source, the characterization of Antiochus was largely the work of this author. Antiochus has been presented according to the stereotype of the tyrant in the ancient world—a thoroughly negative figure, indeed the most negative in the Greek environment, which prized 'freedom' and 'democracy' as the highest political goods.

Lucian of Samosata wrote several works that deal with the character of tyrants. In a comedy, 'The Downward Journey, or, the Tyrant', typical charges are brought against the tyrant Megapenthes as he is hauled before Minos for eternal judgement:

> After he had *made himself extremely rich*, he did not leave a single form of excess untried, but practised *every sort of savagery and high-handedness* upon his miserable fellow-citizens, ravishing maids, *corrupting boys*, and running amok in every way among his subjects. And for his superciliousness, *his pride, and his haughtiness* toward all he met you could never exact from him a fitting penalty... Then, too, *in the matter of punishments who could describe his cruel inventiveness*? (*Tyrannicide* 26)

The italics indicate points of contact, or potential points of contact, with Antiochus in *4 Maccabees*. Antiochus enriched himself through bribes, a fact that *4 Maccabees* has retained in abbreviated form from his source. Antiochus did not merely execute his enemies, as a legitimate king would have done—he is portrayed as the inventor of cruel torments (10.16) and the ringmaster of the arena in which the martyrs suffer such brutal torments. Torture was portrayed as the day-to-day business of tyrants, who had to maintain their rule by fear and force (see Seneca, *De ira* 2.23.1; Thucydides, *Histories* 6.57.4; Diogenes Laertius, *Lives* 9.26, 58-60; Cicero, *Tusculun Disputations* 2.52). The image of Antiochus 'sitting...on a certain high place' surrounded by his 'armed soldiers' (5.1) is taken from ancient depictions of tyrants, who indeed can never go far from their ever-present armed guards.

Tyrants are frequently depicted as paedophiles. They are characterized as indulging their sensual pleasures to excess (Plato, *Republic* 573D), and love of young men or boys represents the extreme of their excesses. Frequently such outrages led to the tyrant's downfall, or at least brought him grief (Aristotle, *Politics* 5.8.9 [1311b]; Cicero, *Tusculun Disputations* 5.60; Thucydides, *Histories* 6.54.2-4). Heininger (1989: 52) suggests plausibly that some hint of this lurks behind the tyrant's admiration of the seven brothers, which several times speaks of their beauty or handsome appearance (8.3-5a).

The association of the destruction of laws and the reign of tyrants is also very strong in the literature. Antiochus's abrogation of his predecessors' decrees concerning Jewish self-rule by the Torah, and even his attempt to abolish the Jewish Torah personally, fit the stereotype. Dionysius of Halicarnassus (*Roman Antiquities* 4.41.2) wrote of Lucius Tarquinius, who, having obtained power, 'confounded and abolished the old customs, the laws, and the whole native form of government, by which the former kings had ordered the commonwealth, and transformed his rule into an avowed tyranny'. After the death of the tyrants, as Lucian (*Tyrannicide* 10) celebrates, 'everything is full of peace, we have all our laws'. Fittingly, the restoration of peace and law-observance is precisely the result of the martyrs' contest with Antiochus (18.4)

Antiochus's character is thus portrayed most negatively. The traditional tyrant typology of the Greek and Hellenistic world already undermines his legitimacy as a ruler. The author's further characterization of him as 'impious' (9.31-32; 10.11; 12.11), as a 'hater of virtue' (11.4), as 'bloodthirsty, murderous, and utterly abominable' (10.17), as unjust (11.6) and shameless (12.11, 13), confirm that his credibility as a speaker will not stand. The very positions he represents will be tainted by his character. Conversely, the views and positions advocated by the martyrs are made credible and reliable by their flawless character. From the preceding chapter it will be clear that the audience would recognize the martyrs as people wholly committed to virtue. This commitment to virtue, to piety and to loyalty toward God and the ancestral law becomes itself the guarantee of the truth of their 'philosophy', as the author explicitly states in 7.9.

Antiochus's Criticism of the Jewish Philosophy

Introducing speeches into narrative was a time-honoured tradition in both historiography (Thucydides, *Histories* 1.21-22) and oratory (Quintilian, *Institutes* 6.1.25-26; 9.2.29-30). The criterion for such speeches was not absolute accuracy, but appropriateness: we need not suppose that the author had access to the actual words of Antiochus, but rather that his hearers would have recognized his words as appropriate for a Gentile critic of Judaism. Antiochus is given a complete deliberative speech, in which he seeks to persuade Eleazar (and, indirectly, the rest of his Jewish captives) to abandon their native customs and accept his way of life. He uses many of the 'categories of persuasion' found in deliberative speeches and listed in rhetorical handbooks. Anaximenes, for example, listed the following (Aristotle, *Rhetorica ad Alexandrum* 1.1421b,21–1422b,12): 'that which is right (*dikaion*), lawful (*nomimon*), expedient or beneficial (*sumpheron*), honourable (*kalon*), pleasant (*hēdus*), easy (*radion*), feasible (*dunaton*) and necessary (*anagkaion*)'. The opposites, of course, could be used as 'categories of dissuasion'. Antiochus argues largely from the 'pleasant', 'beneficial' (a notably Stoic category) and 'necessary' (this being the same word as 'compulsion'—Antiochus himself provides the necessity), whereas the martyrs cling to the 'right', 'lawful' and 'honourable' while countering Antiochus' arguments concerning what is truly 'expedient' and 'necessary'.

Antiochus begins his speech by claiming that observing 'the religion of the Jews' is incompatible with being 'a philosopher' (5.7). The Jewish way of life, for him, is rather a 'vain opinion concerning the truth' and a 'foolish philosophy' (5.10, 11). The Jewish law seems to him to be opposed to Nature, which provides the highest law. Antiochus' criticism of the ethnic customs and laws of the Jews rests on the Stoic critique of all human laws when set against the universal law of Nature. Dio Chrysostom (*Orations* 80.5-7; cf. Epictetus, *Discourses* 1.13.5) gave expression to this tendency to relativize, even reject, human laws and seek out the higher law that is not to be found in any national law code:

> Even now men say that justice resides in whatever laws they themselves, luckless creatures that they are, may frame or else inherit from others like themselves. But the law which is true and binding and plain to behold they neither see nor make a guide for their life. So at noon, as it were, beneath the blazing sun, they go about with torches and flambeaux in their hands, ignoring the light of heaven but following smoke if it shows even a slight glint of fire. Thus, while the law of Nature is abandoned and eclipsed with you, poor unfortunates that you are, tablets and statute books and slabs of stone with their fruitless symbols are treasured by you.

This philosophical approach is combined with the more general opinion of Judaism as a 'foolish superstition' rather than an honourable philosophy. Plutarch (*Superstition* 8 [*Moralia* 169C]), for example, criticized the strict observance of the Sabbath, which led Jews to refuse even to defend themselves on that day, as a 'cowardly excuse', the result of being 'fast bound in the toils of superstition as in one great net'. Jewish abstinence from pork (the 'most proper type of meat' according to Plutarch) was the frequent target of contempt, ridicule and misunderstanding (Plutarch, *Table-Talk* 5.1 [*Moralia* 669E-F]; Tacitus, *Histories*

5.4.3; Juvenal, *Sat.* 14.98-99; Josephus, *Apion* 2.137; cf. *Letter of Aristeas* 128-130). While eating pork would be regarded as a 'shameful' thing according to the ethnic, human law of the Jews, Nature passed no such judgment on the flesh of this animal. While Eleazar was observing his local customs, he is charged by Antiochus with an injustice (*adikon*) against Nature, showing ingratitude and doing her an injury by spurning her gifts (5.8-9).

In addition to this more philosophical critique, Antiochus adds as a motivation the pressure he is about to put on Eleazar. The English words for 'tortures' and 'compulsion' or 'necessities' can all be represented by a single Greek word. It would be expedient for Eleazar to follow the course of action proposed by Antiochus, for thus he would preserve his life and escape great harm (5.10-12). In Antiochus's eyes, Judaism is not a philosophy worth dying for since it is a 'vain [empty] opinion'. It becomes only sensible to give this up for the pleasant way of life offered by accommodation to and assimilation into Hellenism. This may indeed be getting close to the deliberations within a certain segment of the audience of *4 Maccabees* as well, for whom it appeared expedient to yield to the subtler pressures of the dominant Greek culture.

Antiochus concludes his speech by trying to help Eleazar accept the transgression of his law: 'if there is some power watching over this religion of yours, it will excuse you from any transgression that arises out of compulsion' (5.13). Hadas (1953: 171) suggests that this 'argument was a cogent one, and must have weighed heavily with our author's audience, who had somehow to adjust themselves to the demands of their environment'. Aristotle, indeed, recognized that authorities did not punish 'evil...done under compulsion' (*Nicomachean Ethics* 3.5.7 [1113b24-29]), and that pardon was bestowed 'when a man does something wrong through fear of penalties that impose too great a strain on human nature, and that no one could endure' (3.1.7 [1110a23-25]). Nevertheless, there were certain acts which 'a man cannot be compelled to do, and rather than do them he ought to submit to the most terrible death' (*Nicomachean Ethics* 3.1.8 [1110a25-28]). It is the task of Eleazar to explain to Antiochus, and more especially to the audience, why every transgression of the Torah belonged to this latter category.

Eleazar's Defence of Jewish Philosophy
Speaking for all 'who have been persuaded to govern [their] lives by the divine law' (5.16), Eleazar responds to the tyrant's threats of torture that no compulsion could be greater than the necessity of obedience. In

effect, Eleazar claims that virtue itself is the foremost compulsion, and no other force would ever weigh so heavily on the pious Jew's mind. Eleazar's commitment to obey the laws of his people is a familiar aspect of the virtue of 'justice' (*dikaiosunē*). Aristotle commented that 'to righteousness it belongs…to preserve ancestral customs and institutions and the established laws' (*On Virtue and Vices* 5.2). Prominent among the 'claims of righteousness' is 'piety' (*eusebeia*), or 'duties toward the gods', the virtue that rises to prominence in the martyr stories.

Eleazar maintains, against Antiochus's relegation of the Torah to the level of human law, that the origin of the Torah was divine (5.16, 25-26). There is no explicit defence of this proposition (as one would expect were the book addressing Gentile readers), but there is something of a functional demonstration: the fact that the Torah teaches every virtue and enables the devout to cling to virtue in the face of such overwhelming external attacks points to its divine origin. Eleazar's heroic willingness to die for preserving obedience to divine law rather than transgress it for the sake of human laws recalls the praiseworthy yet tragic figure of Antigone (cf. Sophocles, *Antigone* 447-70), who also faced execution for the transgression of a tyrant's law on account of her commitment to the laws of the gods. Such obedience was not only a debt owed God, but also to the nation, whose 'reputation for piety' was at stake (5.18) and to the ancestors, who had pledged loyalty to the Torah on their own behalf and on behalf of their descendants (5.29; cf. Exod. 24.3, 7).

The lines that follow have engendered considerable disagreement among scholars: 'do not suppose that it would be a petty sin if we were to eat defiling food; to transgress the law in matters either small or great is of equal seriousness, for in either case the law is equally despised' (5.19-21). A number of scholars assert that Eleazar agrees here with rabbinic statements concerning 'greater' and 'lesser' sins, correcting the Stoic notion that all sins are equal (cf. *SVF* 1.224: 'transgressions are to be considered equal'; Diogenes Laertius, *Lives* 7.120; Cicero, *Paradoxa* 3.1.20; Horace, *Satires* 1.3.120-121). Others, however, argue that Eleazar does not support the distinction between 'petty' and 'serious' transgressions, attributing such evaluations to Antiochus and not to himself.

The rabbinic view, while admitting a gradation of commandments, in fact promoted the keeping of all commands of the Torah:

> be heedful of a light precept as of a weighty one, for thou knowest
> not the recompense of reward of each precept; and reckon the loss

> through [the fulfilling of] a precept against its reward, and the
> reward [that comes] from transgression against its loss (*Abot* 2.1).

Eleazar, while speaking of a distinction between 'small' and 'great' transgression, in fact does not allow dietary regulations to be classified as 'small' matters. Indeed, he even goes so far as to claim that transgressing in 'small' or 'great' matters is 'of equal seriousness' (*isodunamon*), employing terminology very much at home in Stoic discussions of the equality of errors. While allowing, then, for the possibility of a classification of the prescriptions of the Torah as 'smaller' and 'greater' matters, the most important thing for him is that every transgression shows an equal contempt for the Law, and hence the Lawgiver. Every transgression is thus equally to be avoided. *4 Maccabees* and *Pirke Abot* are not functionally distant from the Stoic doctrine: while the laws themselves may be weighted differently, the gravity of transgression remains constant just as the reward for keeping a commandment will always outweigh the cost.

Eleazar is particularly concerned with not showing contempt himself for the Torah or its author, and with not bringing shame and ridicule upon the Jewish nation. In essence, he is concerned with preserving the honour of God's name, which is fundamentally what is at stake in the public arena that Antiochus has arranged. Hadas (1953: 119-20, 167-69) notes the gravity of a transgression committed publicly (*bᵉparhesya*). Such an act would bring open contempt upon God, and so must be avoided at all costs: 'it is no mere point of personal pride when Eleazar objects that he will be laughed at for violating his principles...and no bravado when he expresses indignation at the proffered ruse by which he would only *appear* to be transgressing'. Dishonouring God, or being the cause of such contempt, carries fearful consequences. This issue becomes even more important in the martyrdom of the seven brothers in the scenes that follow (e.g., 13.13-16).

As a positive defence of the Law, Eleazar cites the role of the Torah as the instructor (*paideutēs*, 5.34) of virtue. This essentially covers in a brief space a major point of the philosophical discussion that opened the discourse, where the Torah educated the mind and enabled it to overcome the voices of the passions and choose virtuous action (cf. 2.21-23):

> You scoff at our philosophy as though living by it were irrational,
> but it teaches us self-control, so that we master all pleasures and
> desires, and it also trains us in courage, so that we endure any suf-
> fering willingly; it instructs us in justice, so that in all our dealings

we act impartially, and it teaches us piety, so that with proper reverence we worship the only living ['existing', Gk *onta*] God (5.22-
24).

Eleazar claims that Jewish philosophy is indeed a life in accordance with
right reasoning (*meta eulogistias*, a special term in Stoicism: *SVF* 3.264,
268; Epictetus, *Discourses* 1.11.17-20; see Klauck 1989a: 712). The proof
of this claim is the virtue that observance of the Torah develops in the
lives of its pupils. Keeping the law, then, is truly advantageous
(*sumpheron*), despite Antiochus's asseverations to the contrary, for it leads
to virtue. As the author will go on to claim, the 'advantage' of Torah-
observance extends beyond the circumstances of this life, bringing eternal life in the presence of God in its train (9.8, 22; 10.15, etc.).

Eleazar's definitions of the virtues follow the general trends of Greek
and Latin ethical writings (cf. Cicero, *Rhetorica ad Herennium* 3.2.3).
The new focus on piety, while not a distinctively Jewish virtue, is especially useful for the promotion of Judaism. The exclusive claim made
here, that the Torah enables the Jew 'with proper reverence [to] worship the only living [existing] God', echoes discussions of piety in the
Letter of Aristeas, where the law protects Jews from falling under the
'vain opinions' of other nations, so that they revere 'the one and
mighty God above the whole of creation' (139; cf. 142). Eleazar indirectly throws back at the polytheist Antiochus the charge of 'holding a
vain opinion concerning the truth' (5.10). It is the Gentile who does
not worship the One God whose mind is indeed 'alienated from the
truth' (*3 Macc.* 4.16), who is trapped by 'vain opinions'.

All of these arguments—the compelling power of justice, the necessity of honouring the divine Law, and the virtuous life that results from
following the Torah—are marshalled by Eleazar to support his stance of
refusing to eat the pork:

> Therefore we do not eat defiling food; for since we believe that
> the law was established by God, we know that in the nature of
> things [or, according to nature] the Creator of the world in giving
> us the law has shown sympathy toward us. He has permitted us to
> eat what will be most suitable for our lives, but he has forbidden
> us to eat meats that would be contrary to this (5.25-26).

Eleazar must instruct Antiochus concerning what is truly beneficial,
allowable and forbidden, since his own reasonings have led him to
approve what the Torah prohibits. This comes very close to the
philosopher's definition of freedom and slavery in Dio Chrysostom
(*Orations* 14.18):

> we define freedom as the knowledge of what is allowable and
> what is forbidden, and slavery as ignorance of what is allowed and
> what is not. According to this definition, there is nothing to pre-
> vent the Great King, while wearing a very tall tiara upon his head,
> from being a slave and not being allowed to do anything that he
> does; for every act that he performs will bring a penalty and be
> unprofitable.

The pious Jew is the free person; the tyrant shows himself to be a slave
through ignorance of the divine law.

Eleazar scores an important point for the Jewish law over against the
'universal law' of the Stoics. For the Stoic, the principle that guided life
was to live 'according to Nature' (*kata phusin*). 'Nature' here refers to
the divine ordering principle that 'shapes [all things] towards their
proper ends' (Staniforth 1964: 16). To live 'according to Nature' was
to act so as to fulfil the goal proper to one's constitution. Human
beings, containing a spark of the divine mind, are suited to the life of
reason and virtue: being dominated by passions and participating in
vice are not proper to 'Nature' as far as the human being is concerned.
Living 'according to Nature' means following reason rather than being
carried away by faulty opinions or passions. This brings one to life's
goal (*telos*), namely virtue and happiness.

The Torah, Eleazar declares, had its origin in the Creator of the uni-
verse—the divine mind itself. To know what is proper and suitable for
human nature, one needs only to consult the Torah, which Divine
Providence had provided for this very purpose. Any transgression of
the Torah, conversely, must be reckoned a transgression of that highest
law, as a departure from living 'according to Nature', and hence a
departure from virtue and happiness. Moreover, as the author would
go on to show, Nature is, by itself, a fallible guide to virtue. Nature
will lead the brothers and mother to transgress for the sake of familial
affection (cf. 15.25); the Torah, however, makes it possible for them to
discern what was truly most fitting, and so enables them to remain
firm. Jewish dietary regulations are thus defended as revealing what
foods are truly suitable for human life, and what are not suitable (cf. the
more explicit explanation in Philo, *Spec. Leg.* 4.100). Eleazar therefore
resolves to die rather than betray the Jewish philosophy, which is
divine in origin, the instructor of every virtue, and the sign of God's
compassion for God's creation—God's provision for the freedom of the
human mind, teaching what things are lawful and suitable, and what
things are not.

Effect on the Audience

The author hopes that Eleazar's 'words of divine philosophy', made 'credible' by his willingness to die for it, will strengthen their 'loyalty to the law' (7.9). He bolsters Eleazar's arguments with the reminder that the Torah-centered mind is alone capable of full commitment to virtue, returning thus to his protreptic purpose at the close in 7.17-19. On the strength of Eleazar's example, the author boldly affirms that 'as many as attend to religion with a whole heart, these alone are able to control the passions of the flesh, since they believe that they, like our patriarchs Abraham and Isaac and Jacob, do not die to God, but live to God' (7.18-19). An exclusive claim to virtue (the corollary of mastering the 'passions of the flesh') is made for the devout followers of the Torah. The less specific 'religion' is given clear definition both by what precedes (it is the religion of Eleazar) and by what follows (it is the religion of the Jewish patriarchs). As Redditt (1983: 258) correctly observes, all that is required for the rational faculty (*logismos*) to fulfil its divinely-appointed function is unswerving commitment to the Torah. The main impact that the author seeks for Eleazar's example to have on the hearers is to move them to hold to the Jewish way of life more vigorously.

An important support for this commitment is the conviction that death does not spell the end of the life of the righteous person. 7.19 (far from being an interpolation modelled after 16.25) announces a theme that runs throughout *4 Maccabees* as an explicit motivation for persevering in obedience to the Torah (9.8-9, 32b; 10.11, 15; 12.18; 13.14-17; 15.2-4; 16.23; 17.5, 12). The removal of death's sting is a prerequisite to absolute commitment to virtue also in the Stoic school (cf. Seneca, *De constantia* 8.3). This conviction has a powerful effect on the deliberations of the pious mind. If obedience to the Torah leads to eternal advantage, it is reasonable to endure any temporary disadvantage in order to keep that eternal possession secure; conversely, no worldly gain could compensate for the loss of eternal rewards. This becomes an important and explicit factor in the decisions of the seven brothers and their mother to remain steadfast in their loyalty to God through Torah (13.13-17; 15.2-3, 8, 27). One may surmise also that the author hopes it will become an important consideration in the minds of the audience, as they weigh the potential advantages of compromising the Torah for this world against the potential disadvantages of such a policy for the next, eternal world.

Eleazar's defence of the reasonableness of strict Torah-observance is an important vehicle for the author's purpose. In Eleazar's response to Gentile criticism and censure, and in the author's affirmation of the devout person as the realization of the ideal of virtue and freedom, the Torah has become not only a viable philosophy alongside those of the Hellenistic world, but has become the 'whole rule [or "complete standard"] of philosophy' (*holon ton tēs philosophias kanona*, 7.21). What Antiochus ignorantly slandered as a 'vain opinion' and 'foolish philosophy' has been shown, by the perfect fruit it bears in Eleazar, to be the standard by which all philosophy is to be judged (Redditt 1983: 261). The audience should therefore not be moved by the ongoing Gentile criticism of the Jewish way of life, but rather should be confirmed in the conviction that trusting God and walking by the Torah is the surest path to virtue and its rewards.

Rejection of an Alternative Way of Life

In the second 'speech duel', the author turns from Gentile censure of the Jewish way of life to Gentile enticements away from that way of life. The comparison of two courses is a fundamental element of deliberative rhetoric: one must be prepared to show that the course one advocates will result in greater safety and honour than the course urged by one's opponents (cf. Cicero, *Rhetorica ad Herennium* 3.2.3; 3.3.4). Here, it is the enticement of assimilation, and the advantages of adoption of the Greek way of life promised its converts, which the author would have to show truly to be disadvantageous for the Jew. Many in the audience might hear themselves addressed in Antiochus' offer of patronage, and the author hopes that the nobility of the seven brothers who die 'for the sake of piety' will inspire his audience to strengthen their commitment to the Torah as well. He hopes their words and example will move the hearers to avoid the enticements of apostasy, to turn away from the cowardly path of accommodation, and to measure their self respect in terms of their steadfastness in the faith of their ancestors and in their loyalty to the patron–client relationship they enjoy with God.

The Enticements of Assimilation

After his 'defeat' by Eleazar, Antiochus orders that other Hebrew captives be brought forward. The seven brothers and their mother are brought before the king by his guards. The youths are presented as 'handsome, modest, noble and accomplished in every way' (8.3), and Antiochus explicitly admits being 'struck by their appearance and nobility' (8.4) as he opens his speech (8.5a). While Heininger (1989:

52) may be correct in suggesting that the lurid paedophilia connected with ancient tyrant typology lurks behind these remarks, more to the point is Antiochus's recognition that the seven have great potential for a successful life in the Greek culture, as they embody the Greek ideal of the beauty and skill of the male youth.

The tyrant approaches them with an attitude of favour—that is, he is disposed to be their patron or sponsor as they enter the 'Greek way of life'. It was part of the stereotyped presentation of tyrants to portray them using both threats and promises, both pain and favour, to accomplish their purpose (Heininger 1989: 51), but the situation of the hearers must have resonated strongly with the tyrant's promises. Antiochus begins not with coercive threats but promises—offers which would be regarded as quite generous in the eyes of the dominant culture. He invites the youths to enjoy his 'friendship' (8.5b), by which he means his patronage. The king's 'friend' was a special client of the king, one who enjoyed a rather immediate access to the king's favour and the resources from which the king might make a timely response to any request.

In the ancient world, patronage was 'the practice which constituted the chief bond of human society' (Seneca, *De beneficiis* 1.4.2). A powerful patron was the most valuable resource, since from him, or through his association with other powerful figures, one could acquire opportunities for wealth, land, office and advancement that would otherwise be completely out of reach. A patron would dispense 'favour' (*charis*); a client would return 'favour' in the form of 'gratitude' (also *charis*). More than a mere feeling, 'gratitude' in the ancient world meant the duty to honour one's patron, to spread his or her reputation, to remain loyal to that patron and his or her 'friends' and clients, and to provide whatever services might be required by that patron (hence, obedience in 8.6b). Antiochus invites the youths to 'trust' him (*pisteusate*), that is, to rely on him fully for their future, and thus be emboldened to break with their inner-Jewish networks of patronage. Antiochus returns again to the 'category of persuasion' called 'the pleasant' (*hēdun*; cf. Aristotle, *Rhet. ad Alex.* 1.1421b21-1422b12; Aristotle, *Nicomachean Ethics* 2.3.7 [1104b31-32]), urging the brothers to 'enjoy' their youths, an enjoyment virtually assured by the personal patronage of the king. He warns them not to rouse his anger through disobedience (8.9), anger being the natural response of one who has desired to benefit others, but who is instead insulted by them (so Aristotle, *Rhetoric* 2.2.8)—here, by watching his favour spurned with contempt and his decrees disregarded.

Jews in the Hellenized cities of their Diaspora faced some severe challenges in the attempt to secure advancement in the Greek world and to develop patron–client relationships with the rich and powerful who were not of their race. The dietary regulations of the Torah and the strict prohibitions against idolatry made mingling with most potential patrons quite difficult. The Jews prized the well-disposed Gentile patrons they could attract (such as those who built synagogues for them, and became benefactors to the whole Jewish community). The careers of several apostate (or relaxed) Jews like Tiberius Alexander (Philo's nephew) testify to the worldly benefits of assimilation. It must have been extremely tempting for many Jews, when wealth and advancement were so close at hand, to succumb to the enticements and purchase, at the cost of strict observance of the Torah, safety and advantage in the Greek world. The prominence of this enticement may be reflected in Antiochus's repetition of his offer of personal patronage to the last brother and his promises of a brilliant career in his government (12.5).

This gives particular poignancy to both the hypothetical and actual responses of the brothers in this discourse, by means of which the author addressed the concerns and aspirations that weighed heavily in his audience's deliberations. Some of them may have had equal promise for success in the 'Greek way of life'. How could the author pull them back to desire the Jewish way of life? Just as the author had sought to disarm the sting of the dominant culture's negative evaluation of Judaism as a shameful, barbaric superstition (*mania*, 8.5), so he also sought to relegate the honours that the dominant culture offered to a position of little importance. His goal for his audience was very much like that of Seneca for the Stoic wise person:

> In the same spirit in which he sets no value (*nihilo aestimat*) on the honours they have, he sets no value on the lack of honour they show. Just as he will not be flattered if a beggar shows him respect, nor count it an insult if a man from the dregs of the people, on being greeted, fails to return his greeting, so, too, will he not even look up if many rich men look upon him. For he knows that they differ not a whit from beggars. (*De constantia* 13.2)

The 'philosopher of the divine life'—the Jew—is rather to seek honour and avoid shame solely on the basis of loyalty to God and God's Torah, the guide to all virtue.

The Road Not Taken

Having repeated his threats of torture and his argument that 'whatever justice you revere will be merciful to you when you transgress under compulsion' (8.14; cf. 5.13b), Antiochus awaits the brothers' answer. The author tells us at once that they 'nullified' his tyranny with their 'right reasoning' (8.15), but before giving their response he pauses in order to 'consider, on the other hand, what arguments might have been used if some of them had been cowardly and unmanly' (8.16).

He places upon the brothers' lips a speech which, in effect, considers the tyrant's points one by one and assents to them. In this speech, Antiochus's offer of kind treatment, and his threats of severe punishment, persuade the youths to accept the dominant culture's evaluation of their religion as 'vain opinion' and their commitment to the Torah as 'arrogance' (8.19). They accept Antiochus's argument that God will pardon them for transgression, since they do it not voluntarily, but under compulsion (8.22, 25). This hypothetical response to Antiochus bears a strong resemblance to Ismene's sensible but cowardly attempts to dissuade her sister Antigone from disobeying the king's laws, even if obedience to the mortal meant disobedience to the gods (who would surely forgive those who act under constraint; Sophocles, *Antigone* 58-68). So also the brothers, if they had followed this route, would have preferred 'safety' to a 'noble death' for some higher ideal, and thus embodied the essence of cowardice (cf. Aristotle, *On Virtue and Vices* 6.5-6).

The final words of this speech sum up the dilemma facing the author's own audience: 'Why does such contentiousness excite us and such a fatal stubbornness please us, when we can live in peace if we obey the king?' (8.26). The Jews, indeed, could gain this life of 'peace' if they would but join in the idolatrous commitments of their neighbours and no longer maintain the separateness that excited suspicion, prejudice and, ultimately, hostility. The author, however, brands this alternative course—the course of accommodation, of yielding both to the promises and pressures of the dominant culture—as cowardice, which was universally regarded as a base and shameful vice. He no doubt hopes that his strong censure of the 'road not taken' by the martyrs (and the stirring speech that follows as they reveal their true resolve) would shame the wavering among the audience into not yielding to these promises or pressures. He hopes it might rouse community support for enforcing the social sanction of dishonour as the reward for those leaning toward, or crossing the line into, violation of the Torah for the sake of the enjoyment of the Greek world's honours and pleasures.

Moreover, by presenting the possibility of deliberation over whether or not to yield, the author makes it clear that such transgression truly would be voluntary, since freely chosen, and therefore perhaps not as unambiguously pardonable as Antiochus has suggested. The prominence of this argument, and the author's rejection of it, has suggested plausibly to Hadas (1953: 171; cf. S.K. Williams 1975: 173) that it was a particularly keen one facing the audience. Some segment of the Jewish community had posited, perhaps, that the future of the religion itself depended on making some concessions now, and that, since it was a matter of survival, small transgressions would be pardoned. For the author, however, any contempt shown for the Torah was infinitely more dangerous than any disadvantage that the hostile Gentile could inflict in this life. This would ultimately form an important part of the brothers' motivation for endurance unto death (13.13-17). Just as the brothers, being complete devotees of virtue, did not even consider such things seriously, so the author hopes that his hearers will cease to contemplate the capitulation that represents an unbecoming lack of virtue.

The Response of Courage
Having paused to censure the path of accommodation, the author presents the brother's actual, courageous response. They speak with 'one voice together, as from one mind' (8.29), thus expressing at the outset that unity of soul in their mutual dedication to piety which will be featured later in the author's encomium. Unanimity, indeed, is frequently praised as a civic virtue (cf. Dio Chrysostom, *Orations* 48), something which 'exists between good men' whose 'wishes are steadfast, and do not ebb and flow like the tide, and they wish for just and expedient ends, which they strive to attain in common' (Aristotle, *Nicomachean Ethics* 9.6.3 [1167b3-9]). The seven brothers have indeed been united by their common desire to preserve justice (to which belongs the keeping of ancestral laws) and to seek one another's highest advantage, which is not to be found in worldly advancement at the cost of God's favour. Once more, the hearers are to emulate this mutual support and commitment to virtue.

The brothers announce their willingness 'to die rather than transgress our ancestral commandments' (9.1). Like Eleazar, they also recognize that they are the safeguards of the honour of the ancestors, and must act so as to bring no shame upon them (9.2; cf. 5.29). They reject the tyrant as their counsellor, and with him all his arguments concerning the benefits of assimilation, for to the noble of heart ensuring safety through transgression (i.e. dishonourable means) is more grievous than pain and death (9.4). Here again the author engages the topic of courage, namely, choosing death over any safety gained at the cost of a disgraceful retreat. Such transgression of the Torah would rob the youths of the 'prize of virtue', and so, like Socrates, they prefer to renounce the worldly, temporary honours that excite the majority of people and live for virtue (Plato, *Gorgias* 526d-527b). This will gain for them a greater, longer-lasting advantage than Antiochus's patronage ever could.

   At the conclusion of their response, the brothers appeal to the concept of divine retribution. This introduces the categories of eternal advantage and disadvantage into the deliberations, making the martyrs' choice of resistance all the more reasonable:

> we, through this severe suffering and endurance, shall have the prize of virtue and shall be with God, on whose account we suffer; but you, because of your bloodthirstiness toward us, will deservedly undergo from the divine justice eternal torment by fire (9.8-9).

The brothers go on to encourage one another not to fear the tyrant, but rather to fear the God 'who gave us our lives' and who threatens more grievous punishment for 'those who transgress the commandment of God' (13.13-16). The loss which would be incurred by violating the Torah and breaking faith with God is infinitely greater than any loss incurred by violating human decrees or affronting human customs for the sake of remaining faithful; conversely, the rewards to be enjoyed in God's presence far outweigh the transitory pleasures of Hellenization that would be purchased at so high a cost. Truly reasoning according to 'the truth of the beneficial' (*to sumpheron*, 5.11), then, actually requires fidelity to the Torah unto death if such were to be called for. *4 Maccabees* here shares with Wisdom of Solomon (cf. 6.17-20) the conviction that immortality is the prize of virtue, the result of following that Wisdom that is revealed in the Torah.

   The 'philosopher of divine life' (7.7), like Socrates, seeks to live for the approval of this higher, eternal court, whose verdict will be rendered on the basis of how closely one has allowed the Torah to form virtue in the soul; he or she may also be assured that the enemies of virtue (11.4) will be arraigned before this court, made to realize their error, and punished for their vice. The brothers, therefore, reject the tyrant's offer of personal patronage (to be gained at the cost of transgression), and accept from him the only fitting 'favour'—the 'opportunity to show our endurance for the law' (11.12). The audience is instructed that the most valuable favour they can receive from the dominant culture is the chance to show themselves complete with regard to their dedication to God's law and their virtue, to be tried and proven in their commitment to virtue (cf. Seneca, *De constantia* 3.4; 9.3; Epictetus, *Discourses* 1.6.37).

The author presents the importance to these brothers of being found worthy of the patriarch Abraham: 'Remember whence you came, and the father by whose hand Isaac would have submitted to being slain for the sake of religion' (13.12). He reminds the audience that it is not their task to live up to the expectations of the Gentile world, but rather to the models of piety that constitute their own ancestry. Being found worthy of the Gentiles' honour is not nearly so valuable as proving oneself worthy to be a descendant of Abraham, for the opinion of the ancestors is eternal, not temporal: 'If we so die, Abraham and Isaac and Jacob will welcome us, and all the fathers will praise us' (13.17). To barter such eternal renown for transitory acceptance among the ignorant Gentiles becomes unthinkable. The final exhortation, also, is directed at the audience. As the brothers cry out to one another, 'do not put us to shame, brother, or betray the brothers who have died before us' (13.18), the audience addressed by the discourse is also being called so to live as to preserve the honour of such martyrs. Indeed, their death would have little meaning if, only a few generations later, their descendants, whose faith they preserved at such cost to themselves, were relinquishing the precious Torah under far less pressure.

Effect on the Audience

The seven episodes of the martyrdom of the seven brothers accomplish far more than telling a story or multiplying examples for the philosophical thesis with which the work began (1.1), and for which the martyrs were introduced as supporting examples (1.8). In the words of Antiochus one hears the enticements that exercised a pressure on the Jewish community to assimilate and enjoy the wealth, associations and advancement that would follow, as well as the threat of deprivation and even harm should the Jews persist in remaining separate for the sake of God and their Law. In the voices of the martyrs, however, one hears inducements to persevere in piety, to reject the opinions and evaluations of the dominant culture as based on ignorance of what is truly right and what wrong, and, instead, to seek recognition from God and

the community of Abraham's children, who understand what is honourable and what censurable. The path of accommodation, of yielding
to the dominant culture's promises and pressures, is the path of cowardice and disgrace. It is, moreover, the path of eternal disadvantage
since it would arouse God's wrath and judgment upon the disloyal
client (cf. 13.15). Even though it might mean temporary disadvantages,
loyalty to God through observance of the Torah is the path to greater
advantage: the martyrs' words, confirmed and made credible by their
actions, reveal the policy approved by God for the Jewish audience.

Promotion of the Jewish Way of Life

In the two 'speech duels', the author of *4 Maccabees* has gone far to promote the Jewish way of life for his audience. In Eleazar's exchange
with Antiochus, the author has answered common Gentile criticisms of
the Jewish Torah and affirmed its essential value as the divinely-given
educator in every virtue and in living in accordance with what is suitable for human beings. In the exchange of the seven brothers, the
author has shown that acceptance of assimilation into the dominant
Greek culture, while promising temporal advantages, is actually the
path to eternal loss and disgrace (even disgrace in this life, according to
Eleazar, as Jews abandon their reputation for piety and put their ancestors to shame). A third important component of his encouragement of
the audience to hold fast to Torah-observance comes in the form of the
mother's exhortations to her seven sons. These stirring addresses also
function as direct exhortation of the hearers, who have also become the
children of this 'mother of the nation' (15.29).

The Mother's Exhortation to her Children: The Noble Contest
Because of her mastery of the power of maternal affection for the sake
of piety, the author praises the mother as 'mother of the nation, vindi-
cator of the law and champion of religion' (15.29), whose endurance is
the crowning achievement of the author's demonstration from examples. Noteworthy is the author's naming her 'mother of the nation',
rather than simply of the seven brothers. She becomes in this way also
the benefactor of the audience, since the preservation of their religion
is due to her firmness, as well as a maternal figure who unites the
whole ethnic body of Jews into one family. This reinforces the point
that the audience should embody the seven brothers' unity and mutual
encouragement in virtue (see discussion of 'Fraternal Affection' in

Chapter 3). Her words summon the audience, as well as the seven brothers, to the 'noble contest':

> My sons, noble is the contest to which you are called to bear wit-
> ness for the nation. Fight zealously for our ancestral law...
> Remember that it is through God that you have had a share in the
> world and have enjoyed life, and therefore you ought to endure
> any suffering for the sake of God. For his sake also our father
> Abraham was zealous to sacrifice his son Isaac, the ancestor of our
> nation; and when Isaac saw his father's hand wielding a knife and
> descending upon him, he did not cower. Daniel the righteous was
> thrown to the lions, and Hananiah, Azariah and Mishael were
> hurled into the fiery furnace and endured it for the sake of God.
> You too must have the same faith in God and not be grieved
> (16.16-22).

[handwritten margin note: reciprocity in piety. See Aristotle on what is due the gods. (below)]

The author again introduces the image of the 'contest' (*agōn*), using it in the manner of philosophers, for whom life itself is a contest in which 'a person is to prove noble or base' (Plato, *Republic.* 10.8 [608b]; cf. *Gorgias* 526D-E). This encounter with the Gentile world, however, is a contest in which nobility and distinction can be won—not, as some may think, by joining in the Greek way of life, but rather by remaining firm and loyal to the divine law and its training in virtue.

The Jewish audience, like the seven brothers, has been called by God in order to 'bear witness for the nation'. Eleazar and the seven are acutely aware that the honour of their nation, their ancestors and their God depends on their testimony: will they bear a noble witness or show an unbecoming spectacle of weakness and cowardice? The philosopher as a witness (*martus*) is not unique to *4 Maccabees*. Epictetus (*Discourses* 1.29.44-49) makes use of this potent metaphor when describing the duty of the 'educated person', that is, the Stoic. For Epictetus, the philosopher's confession of his or her philosophy, and his or her testimony to that philosophy in actions, is itself a source of hon-our: to bear a bad witness is the only disgrace worth considering. So for the 'philosopher of the divine life', the Jew, honour rests in bearing a courageous witness of loyalty to God, dishonour in breaking faith with the Divine Patron. Eleazar offers a model testimony both in word and deed, not yielding to the low opinion the Gentile world holds of his philosophy, but defending its credibility with argument and blood. The audience is summoned in this stirring speech to 'go and do likewise'.

[handwritten margin note: 16¹⁶]

At this point the mother reminds her audience of the debt of grati-tude owed to God: existence itself is a benefit from God. In the words of Aristotle, 'no one could ever render [the gods] the honour they

[handwritten margin note: 16¹⁸⁻¹⁹]

deserve, and a man is deemed virtuous if he pays them all the regard he can' (*Nicomachean Ethics* 8.14.4 [1163b16-18]). Failure to revere this debt of gratitude to God is in effect a fundamental violation of virtue: 'not to return gratitude for benefits is a disgrace, and the whole world counts it as such' (Seneca, *De Beneficiis* 3.1.1). No honour could ever be gained if it is based on this poor foundation, namely, violation of God's Law, a return of disobedience where service is due. The hearers, like the seven brothers, are alive because of God's gift: they must remember this debt and reflect their gratitude to the Giver in their every choice and act.

The mother adduces a list of examples from the sacred history of Israel, all of which demonstrate the proper 'faith' toward God. Abraham appears again at the head of the list: the patriarch of the Jewish people was himself willing to sacrifice his son Isaac for the sake of obedience to God, and Isaac, the 'prototype of the willing victim' (O'Hagan 1974: 115), did not cower. The explanation of this resolution in the face of death must be that 'those who die for the sake of God live to God' (16.25): a similar explanation is introduced into the Abraham story by the author of Hebrews (Heb. 11.19). Daniel was cast into the lion's den on account of his refusal to modify his piety according to the decrees of the Persian king. The three young men were cast into the furnace on account of their refusal to compromise their exclusive devotion to their God. Just as the resolve of these three did not depend on the prospect of deliverance but rather on their absolute loyalty, so the resolve of the seven brothers is to be built on their commitment to virtue and to remain loyal to God. The importance of the three young men as examples of fidelity to the One God in a hostile environment is underscored by their frequent appearance in this discourse (13.9; 16.3-4; 18.12-13). These were miraculously saved by God from the trials; the Maccabean martyrs are saved through the trials.

The audience is called to 'have the same faith' (16.22), that is, to remain firm in their loyalty and obedience toward God, and in their trust that God will reward God's righteous servants (cf. 17.4) Further, they are not to 'be grieved', as the mother herself refuses to grieve, since the joys of virtue and rewards of loyalty far outweigh the loss and pain suffered in this life at the hands of the ungodly (cf. Josephus, *Apion* 2.217-218, who also looks to life beyond death as the reward for those who live by, or die for, the Torah). Although they also may be subject to loss and deprived of some temporal advantages, the audience must recognize that what they are gaining through their covenant loyalty is much greater. This conviction provides the necessary prospect of greater advantage required for enduring extreme hardship and loss in this life for the sake of religion.

The Mother's Closing Speech
At the close of the book, the author places a second exhortation by the mother that provides an expansion on that training in the Torah which has been held up so frequently and centrally in the martyr's speeches as the cause of their endurance. The mother of the seven is allowed to have a final word as mother of the nation, to supplement her earlier exhortations (16.16-23) and the author's explicit exhortation to the audience (18.1-2) with a sort of summation of Jewish domestic instruction for the audience's benefit. They will be dismissed from hearing the discourse to re-enter their own contest with her words ringing in their ears.

The mother reminds her children of the instruction of their father, who fulfilled his obligation to the Torah by teaching them the law (Deut. 4.9; 6.7; 11.19). In this way, she connects the audience with their scriptural heritage and invests the author's exhortation with the authority of the divine oracles:

> He read to you about Abel slain by Cain, and Isaac who was offered as a burnt offering, and about Joseph in prison. He told you of the zeal of Phineas, and he taught you about Hananiah, Azariah, and Mishael in the fire. He praised Daniel in the den of the lions and blessed him. He reminded you of the scripture of Isaiah, which says, 'Even though you go through the fire, the flame shall not consume you'. He sang to you songs of the psalmist David, who said, 'Many are the afflictions of the righteous'. He recounted to you Solomon's proverb, 'There is a tree of life for those who do his will'. He confirmed the query of Ezekiel, 'Shall these dry bones live?' For he did not forget to teach you the song that Moses taught, which says, 'I kill and I make alive: this is your life and the length of your days' (18.11-18).

The mother's earlier speech had already held up the examples of Isaac (Gen. 22.1-19), who valued obedience to God's command more than his own life, Daniel (Dan. 6.1-28), who fulfilled piety in every way rather than alter his devotion to suit the cultural and political climate, and Hananiah, Azariah and Mishael (Dan. 3.1-30), who endured the furnace rather than commit idolatry.

Here, the author adds a brief reference to Abel and Cain (Gen. 4.1-

16). The significance of this story here is not explicitly drawn out, but is nevertheless evident. Abel was known for his piety, offering sacrifices acceptable to God. Cain was a model of impiety, whose sacrifices were not acceptable to God. Cain's hostility towards Abel was born of this experience of frustration and envy, yet God upheld Abel's honour and judged Cain. This primeval story may have been applied, then, to Jews, whose piety pleased God, as they experienced hostility from Gentiles, whose piety was idolatrous. The story may thus serve to sustain the pious Jew as he or she encounters opposition, since the opponents are not only one's own enemies but people under God's disapproval. These opponents stand in dishonour now in God's sight, and, like Cain, act unjustly and will come to grief in the judgment. The author also recalls the endurance of Joseph (Gen. 39.7-23), who refused to violate the prohibition of adultery even though he knew the would-be adulteress would have him sent to prison. So also the hearers should imitate his willingness to suffer deprivation rather than choose what might seem the easier path of transgressing one of God's commands. Finally, the author refers to Phineas, known for his zeal for God (Num. 25.7-13). Rather than permit idolatry and affronts to God in the midst of the Israelite camp, Phineas personally executed the Israelite and his Canaanite concubine. While the examples of Abel, Joseph, Daniel and the three young men point to endurance of hostility from without for the sake of the Torah, the example of Phineas points to internal vigilance against assimilation.

The chain of scriptural quotations admirably supports both the martyrs' decisions as well as the resolve that the author hopes to instil in his audience. Isaiah 43.2 promises protection from the flames for those who are called to pass through the fire. The objective experience of the martyrs stands in some tension with this promise: for them, however, the fire transforms them into immortality (9.22). The psalms of David prepare the righteous for affliction (cf. Ps. 34.19, which is quoted here, so that these negative experiences will not shake their conviction of God's favour and providence, nor undermine the foundations of the Deuteronomistic world-view: afflictions will come, but the rewards laid up for the faithful will make these seem but 'momentary, light afflictions'. Proverbs 3.18 speaks of wisdom as the tree of life for those who hold her fast, but here it is transformed into the promise of life for the righteous. Specifically, the fruit of the tree of life was immortality (Gen. 3.22), which is the reward held ever before the eyes of the Torah-observant.

The quotation from Proverbs is closely connected with the final two. Ezekiel's vision (which comes nearest any mention of resurrection in the whole discourse, and even here is completely muted for the sake of the author's preference of immortality of the soul) speaks of God's ability to breathe new life into the dead (Ezek. 37.1-14). Even though the martyrs are 'burned to the very bones' (*4 Macc.* 6.26), they do not fail to achieve the reward promised to those who keep God's covenant, for God's power extends beyond the confines of this life. The final quotation is a combination of Deut. 32.39 and 30.20. The latter text refers in its context to loving, obeying and holding fast to God—a very appropriate connection with the example of the martyrs: 'Choose life so that you and your descendants may live, loving the Lord your God, obeying him, and holding fast to him; for that means life to you and length of days'. Here the promised life and length of days is no longer limited to living in 'the land', but transferred to immortal life in the presence of God. The former text is from the Song of Moses (an important song in other settings of high tension with society, as in Rev. 15.1-8), which as a whole is singularly appropriate to the narrative of *4 Maccabees*. The Song speaks of God punishing Israel for turning to idols (32.15-25), presumably using their Gentile enemies, as agents of punishment (vv. 21, 27). God, however, vindicates Israel before bringing the Jewish people to complete destruction and has 'compassion on his servants' (32.36-43). To this vindication and vengeance upon Israel's enemies, the final verse adds the note that God purifies the land for God's people (32.43c). This forms a sort of template for *4 Maccabees*, with the martyrs serving as the turning point between wrath and compassion, as well as the medium for purification. The word order in this particular quote is also significant: 'I kill and [*then*] I make alive' provides additional support for the belief in the resurrection of the martyred faithful. The absolute power of God over life, death and the life hereafter should give the audience the ultimate motivation to remain loyal and grateful clients of this great Patron, and not sacrifice that relationship for any transitory advantage. Again, the perspective *sub specie aeternitatis* should have enabled the audience to remain steadfast in defending their way of life, knowing that the final outcome is in the hands of the God they served faithfully.

Conclusion

The impact that the author sought for this discourse to have on the audience is summed up in his direct exhortation to them: 'O Israelite children, offspring of the seed of Abraham, obey this law and exercise piety in every way, knowing that devout reason is master of all emotions, not only of sufferings from within, but also of those from without' (18.1). Encomia often end with a hortatory peroration urging the imitation of the virtues embodied, or the way of life embraced, by the subject of the commemorative address (cf. Dio Chrysostom, *Orations* 29.21; Thucydides, *Histories* 2.43.1-4). So for this author, the philosophical demonstration and the praise of the martyrs should combine to motivate the hearers to follow this exhortation and preserve the Jewish 'philosophy' by maintaining the 'Hebrew way of life' despite all the temporal advantages of abandoning it. The relationship between the author's philosophical thesis and his purpose receives clear expression in these verses: the thesis that 'devout reason is sovereign over the emotions' supports obedience to the Torah, giving a certain self respect to the pious Jews in terms derived from Hellenistic culture and giving obedience to the Torah itself the status of a philosophical ideal.

Antiochus posed a threat that was not unknown to Diaspora Jews— the manner of the threat's presentation was different, but the 'way of life of the Hebrews' was no less threatened by the enticements of joining the dominant culture and reaping the temporal benefits of assimilation; it was no less under fire from the apostates from within, whose defection undermined the value and credibility of the Jewish philosophy, and from the Gentile critics without, who did not regard Judaism as compatible with the pursuit of virtue and excellence. The note of regret with which Tacitus (*Histories* 5.8.2), for example, spoke of the failure of Antiochus' Hellenization program in Jerusalem shows that the audience had to continue to defend their 'philosophy' from detractors and to work to maintain their own dedication and self respect. The audience was called to carry on the contest of these martyrs. Just as Eleazar, the mother and the seven brothers so lived as to vindicate their nation, so the audience was to 'look to God', being sure of God's reward for the faithful, to endure any deprivation as a loss incurred for the sake of piety, and to continue the noble contest of preserving the 'Jewish way of life' in the midst of those who prefer and profess the superiority of the 'Greek way of life'. They were to preserve the achievements of the ancestors in the faith and the martyrs themselves by their own renewed dedication to that way of life, and their commitment to defend it with their lives if called upon so to do.

cf. the epitaphios logos
Pericles' Funeral Oration

Further Reading

On the Characterization of Antiochus as Tyrant
Heininger (1989) has provided a useful study of the author's development of the presentation of Antiochus IV using the elements of the stereotype of the tyrant. The most important primary sources are Lucian, *The Tyrant*, which is a satire on the fate of a tyrant in the underworld, and Lucian, *Tyrannicide*, a mock oration demonstrating the patriotism of those who resist and overthrow a tyrant.

Classical Rhetoric (and 4 Maccabees)
See 'Argumentation in the Graeco-Roman World' in the 'Further Reading' section at the end of Chapter 2.

Gentile Criticisms of Judaism
Gager (1983: 35-112) provides a useful orientation to the primary causes of ancient anti-Judaism and to the classical authors who discuss this topic.

Patronage in the Ancient Mediterranean
Saller (1982) provides an excellent starting point for further investigation of the institution of patronage in the Graeco-Roman world. He offers a careful and detailed study of the institutions and vocabulary of patronage within the Roman system. An article by de Ste Croix (1954) that traces the rise of the patronage system and factions in the Roman Republic would be a helpful supplement. A useful discussion of patronal roles, especially the role of the 'broker', appears in Boissevain (1974), who introduced the term into the vocabulary of patronage.

The importance of patronage as a background to the study of the New Testament texts, and by extension to other 'religious' literature of the later Second Temple period, was established by Danker (1982) in his groundbreaking study of the vocabulary of patronage as seen in honourary inscriptions. His observations from epigraphic evidence lead into a detailed analysis of New Testament usage of the same terms. Crossan (1991) also contains helpful information about Roman patronage and sets Jesus' ministry and message in the context of the proclamation of a new order of patronage. DeSilva (1996a) offers a detailed examination of the Epistle to the Hebrews seen in the light of patronage roles and vocabulary.

Perhaps the most important primary source for Roman patronage is Seneca, *On Benefits (De beneficiis)*, in his *Moral Essays*. This is an especially complete and systematic treatise on the roles and obligations of patrons and clients by a native informant. Also helpful is Dio Chrysostom, *Orations* 31 ('To the Rhodian Assembly'), in which Dio urges the people of Rhodes to show proper gratitude towards their past benefactors, warning against the deleterious effects of insulting them by merely engraving the names of new benefactors on the

statues formerly erected for past patrons. Much can be learned from this oration concerning the obligations of clients. Finally, the tenth book of the *Letters*
of Pliny the Younger include many requests made by Pliny to the emperor
Trajan for favours on behalf of Pliny's own clients, showing the dynamics of
brokerage and clientage.

Quotations from Lucian, Aristotle, Dionysius of Halicarnassus, Plutarch, Dio
Chrysostom, Seneca and Josephus have been taken from the LCL editions;
quotations from the *Letter of Aristeas* have been taken from Hadas (1951); quotations from *Pirke Abot* come from the translation by Danby.

6

THE THEOLOGY OF *4 MACCABEES*

4 Maccabees is valuable not only as a *rapprochement* between Jewish faith
and Hellenistic philosophy, providing a sort of complement to the
works of Philo or the Wisdom of Solomon; it is also remarkable as an
expression of Hellenistic Jewish theology. The author opens for us a
window into the development of Judaism away from Judaean soil, dis-
closing facets of that theological environment, which was also the cra-
dle of the theology of the early Christian mission in the Diaspora.
Generated within the synagogue and prized by the early church, *4
Maccabees* reveals a theology embracing potential points of contact with
Paul, his opponents and other important voices in the New Testament
canon.

God as the Divine Patron

The first-century Graeco-Roman world was a patronal society, one in
which the giving and receiving of benefactions was 'the practice that
constitutes the chief bond of human society' (Seneca, *De beneficiis.*
1.4.2; see deSilva 1996a; Danker 1982; Saller 1982). In a world in
which wealth and property were concentrated into the hands of a very
small percentage of the population, the majority of people often found
themselves in need of assistance in one form or another, and therefore
had to seek the patronage of someone who was better placed in the
world than himself or herself. Patrons might be asked to provide
money, grain, employment, or land; the better-connected persons
could be sought out as patrons for the opportunities they would give
for professional or social advancement (Antiochus himself makes such
an offer of personal patronage to the seven brothers, *4 Macc.* 8.3-7).
One who received such a benefit became a client to the patron,
accepting the obligation to publicize the favour and his or her gratitude

for it, thus contributing to the patron's reputation. The client also accepted the obligation of loyalty to a patron and could be called upon to perform services for the patron, thus contributing to the patron's power. The reception of a gift and the acceptance of the obligation of gratitude are inseparable.

The terms 'grace' (*charis*) and 'faith' (*pistis*), so frequently encountered in 'religious' texts, are also central terms in discussions of the roles and obligations of patrons and clients. 'Grace' (*charis*) had three distinct meanings within this social context. It can refer to the benefactor's favourable disposition toward the petitioner (cf. Aristotle, *Rhetoric* 2.7.2), the actual gift or benefit conferred (cf. 2 Cor 8.19), or the client's gratitude, the necessary and appropriate return for favour shown. A person who received 'grace' (a patron's favour) knew also that 'grace' (gratitude) must be returned. Gratitude involved acting in such a way as to enhance the patron's honour and certainly avoiding any course of action that would bring him or her into dishonour (Aristotle, *Nicomachean Ethics* 8.13.2 [1163b1-5]), as well as intense personal loyalty to the patron, even if that loyalty should lead one to lose one's place in one's homeland, one's physical well-being, one's wealth and one's reputation (Seneca, *Epistulae Morales* 81.27). This was a sacred obligation, and the client who failed to show gratitude appropriately was considered base and impious (Dio Chrysostom, *Orations* 31.37). The greater the benefit bestowed, the greater should be the response of gratitude. 'Faith' (*pistis*) and its related words also receive specific meanings within the context of the patron–client relationship (Danker). To place *pistis* in a patron is to trust him or her to be able and willing to provide what he or she has promised. It means, in effect, to entrust one's cause or future to a patron (cf. 4 *Macc.* 8.5-7), to give oneself over into his or her care. *Pistis* also represents the response of loyalty on the part of the client. Having received benefits from a patron, the client must demonstrate *pistis*, 'loyalty', toward the patron (cf. 4 *Macc.* 16.18-22; 7.19; 15.24; 17.2-3). In this context, then, *pistis* speaks to the firmness, reliability and faithfulness of both parties in the patron–client relationship (or the relationship of 'friends').

In order to give expression to supernatural or unseen realities, people in the ancient world used the language of everyday realities: the world beyond was understood by analogy to known quantities in the world-at-hand. The relationship between human and divine beings, cosmic inferiors and superiors as it were, was expressed in terms of the closest analogy in the world of social interaction, namely patronage, so that there is discussion of 'patron deities' by individuals and groups. The author of *4 Maccabees* shares this view of God, presenting God as the creator of the cosmos (5.25; 11.5) and the highest Patron of the inhabitants of that cosmos. As the giver of life, God claims rightly the gratitude, loyalty and service of all the living. It is specifically the awareness of this debt that motivates the seven brothers, for example, to demonstrate the extreme of gratitude and loyalty: 'let us with all our hearts consecrate ourselves to God, who gave us our lives' (13.13). 'Remember that it is through God that you have had a share in the world and have enjoyed life, and therefore you ought to endure any suffering for the sake of God' (16.18-19). The mother enjoins her sons to show 'loyalty towards God' (*pistis pros ton theon*, 16.22, my translation), just as the faithful ancestors who recognized their obligations to their benefactor and refused to break faith for the sake of avoiding pain (cf. van Henten 1993: 126, who also speaks of *pistis* as the 'faithfulness of the martyr until death').

God's patronage of all humanity, specifically God's gifts of power and authority to human rulers, becomes an important vantage point from which to assess the acts of Gentile rulers. Does the authority honour the Divine Patron who gave him or her the office? Does the ruler's policy reflect the interests of God or does it conflict with God's desires, as when the righteous are oppressed by the Gentile king? The seventh brother claims that Antiochus himself holds his throne by divine gift, and holds him accountable to God for his use of that gift: 'since you have received good things and also your kingdom from God, were you not ashamed to murder his servants and torture on the wheel those who practice religion?' (12.11). Antiochus, having received great benefits from God, acted disloyally toward his Patron by attacking God's faithful clients (the very people he, himself a beneficiary of God's gifts, should protect and assist).

The author of the *Letter of Aristeas* shares the view of this author that all good things come from God, and all authority is dispensed by God. Gentile kings are God's clients ('God...apportions fame and great wealth to kings', *Letter of Aristeas* 224) and should therefore acknowledge this debt of gratitude and use their station to serve God, promote God's purposes and care for God's loyal clients (namely the Jewish people). In the *Letter of Aristeas*, Ptolemy II Philadelphus is a positive model of a Gentile king acting virtuously and justly toward God and God's people. When Ptolemy asks how he might show gratitude to God for the safety of his kingdom, he is advised to grant liberty to the Jews brought as slaves to Egypt by his father, Ptolemy I, 'for the same God who has given them their law guides your kingdom also' (*Letter of Aristeas* 15-16; cf. also 19; 37). Antiochus failed to embody the cardinal virtue of a patronal society, namely gratitude.

The idea of God as Patron and human beings (especially, here, the Jewish people) as God's clients provides the framework for the positive and negative sanctions encouraging obedience to God's Law, promising eternal punishment for those who transgress God's standards of justice and show contempt for the obligations of gratitude and loyal service, but also promising eternal benefactions and final vindication for those who remain firm in their trust and obedience. The author seeks to convince the auditors that honouring God and remaining firm in one's commitment to God is the only reasonable and honourable course; God will thus be known still and continually as Benefactor. Dishonouring God for the sake of acceptance by and assimilation into Greek culture and release from tension (whether the physical tension of the rack or the social tension of identification with a minority group and a suspect people) and becoming clients of the dominant culture leads to the experience of God as avenger of his outraged honour and violated beneficence. This was God's response to Jason (4.19-21), and there is no reason to suppose that affronts to God's honour have become less dangerous (both to the individual and to the covenant community).

God is frequently referred to as 'providence' (*pronoia*, 9.24; 13.19; 17.22); once God is called 'the power watching over' the martyrs (*epoptikē dunamis*, 5.13). These are terms used by Plato (*Timaeus*) and Epictetus (e.g., *Discourses* 3.11.6) to refer to God. While God remains the power that guides the cosmos to its appointed end, watching over and directing creation from outside, God does not remain aloof in this author's conception. First, the image of God as Patron is itself already a personalization of providence: patrons and clients, in the optimal cases, enjoyed face-to-face contact with one another; where this was not possible, clients could at least communicate through writing or intermediaries. As Dupont-Sommer (1939: 40) points out, however, God has 'sympathy' for the human race (5.26). *Sumpatheia* is a key motif in the discussion of the mother's feeling for and with her children (14.13, 14, 18, 20; 15.4, 7, 11). God, as personal creator of the human race, has a similar sympathy for God's creatures. In *4 Maccabees* this sympathy enacts itself in the giving of the Torah, which Dupont-Sommer (1939: 40) calls 'a masterpiece of love and intelligent tenderness'.

Faith in *4 Maccabees*, therefore, cannot be dismissed as 'rather trust in an external Providence than an inner dependence arising from an inward relationship. Faith is not a renewing and life-giving power, but confidence in the providential order' (Maldwyn Hughes, as cited in and affirmed by Townshend 1913: 664). Rather, it is a personal trust in and faithfulness toward God, whose aspect as 'providence' overseeing the cosmos serves to heighten God's value as personal, compassionate Patron. Faith (*pistis*) in this sense brings *4 Maccabees* very close to the meaning of faith in the Epistle to the Hebrews, and to Jewish and early Christian theology in general more than to Greek speculation on the divine.

The Nature of Humanity and the Goal of Life

4 Maccabees presents a concise but complete picture of the essential nature of humanity and the divine order that one must strive to maintain throughout life:

> Now when God fashioned human beings, he planted in them emotions and inclinations, but at the same time he enthroned the mind among the senses as a sacred governor over them all. To the mind he gave the law; and one who lives subject to this will rule a kingdom that is temperate, just, good and courageous (2.21-23).

The author appears to share in a Hellenistic Jewish reading of the creation story that is focused more on God's internal planting in the human rather than the planting of the Garden of Eden. Philo (*Leg. All.* 1.43-55), for example, reads the account of God planting a garden not literally 'as if God were making a place of recreation for himself within the material realm'. Rather, he plants 'virtue in the human race...as an assistant against and warder-off of the diseases of the soul' (1.45). For the author of *4 Maccabees*, God has given a certain order to the human being: the mind is to be subject to the God-given law (the Torah), and is by this means to exercise rule over the emotions and character traits that God has implanted. I have already explored the relationship of this anthropology to the author's opposition to the hardline Stoic doctrine of the passions: the author advocates the maintenance of the God-ordained hierarchy as the life of virtue. Since God created the human person with emotions, passions and inclinations, it is the task of the human being to keep the passions in check so that they may fulfil their God-given purposes but not go beyond their appointed limits. The mind, or reason, is to police the passions, allowing what is in accordance with God's purpose and tempering the passions when they seek to overflow their courses and lead the individual away from virtue or into vice.

How can the mind know what is proper for the passions? God, aware of the human plight, gave the Torah to humanity, so that the mind could distinguish between what was 'suitable' and what was 'forbidden' (5.25-26). Ultimately, then, living 'according to Nature', that is, living in accordance with the ends for which providence has shaped the human creature, is the same as living according to the Torah. As long as the supremacy of reason ('devout' because strictly observant of the Torah) over the passions is maintained, the human being will enjoy a life of virtue, reaping the rewards of living in accordance with nature and suffering none of the injuries that come from allowing vice to possess or mar the soul. Here we may note the promise that attaches to such a life: the author claims for the devotee of the Torah the 'kingship' that belongs to the wise person of Stoic discourse (*SVF* 3.617-19; Diogenes Laertius, *Lives* 7.122). Following the Torah will thus lead to the achievement of the Hellenistic ideal of the sage. Such a claim, again, encourages Jews who have internalized Hellenistic standards of evaluation to place a highly positive value on persevering in their own ancestral tradition.

The author's emphasis on mastery, rather than extirpation, of the passions permits the enjoyment of pleasures, but within God's prescribed limits. The premise upon which this rests is that there are certain higher goods for the human community than the enjoyment of pleasure and avoidance of pain. Lust, for example, is not to be indulged (2.1-6a), for sexual pleasure is limited to its role in nurturing the relationship between husband and wife: sexuality serves a higher, interpersonal end. Gluttony is likewise not to be indulged, for the enjoyment of food is not an end in itself, but has the dual object of sustaining life and creating and sustaining fellowship—hence the condemnation of the 'solitary gourmandizer' (1.27; 2.7). Where the passions are tempered or moderated, however, enjoyment of a meal leads to increased camaraderie. Greed is curbed so that care for the poor may be nurtured—taking thought for the human family must take precedence over indulging any desire (lust, gluttony, greed, or, indeed *superbia*, for which Antiochus is soundly chided in 12.13-14). The author's doctrine of the mastery of the passions includes therefore a keen interest in right human relationships, so that the personal goal for life serves not only an individual but also an interpersonal and social interest.

Human life, therefore, is to be enjoyed, but the human spirit is to remain free from bondage to anything pertaining to the passions. The individual remains free to bear witness to God and God's standards, and to choose the path of virtue over temporary safety, comfort, or pleasure. Ultimately, the author's philosophy seeks the preservation of human dignity by securing freedom from base compulsions from within and from enslavement of the mind from without. No matter how strong the desire, or how fearsome the compulsions, the 'philosopher of divine life' will remain free to choose the course that preserves justice toward God, right relationships toward others, and one's own self-respect.

The Torah, Covenant and Divine Justice

The Torah occupies a central role in *4 Maccabees*. The Torah as the educator or instructor of the mind (2.23; 5.24, 34) is central to the author's thesis, since subservience to the Torah disciplines one in the exercise of reason's mastery over the passions (1.30b–3.18). Indeed, the comparison between *4 Macc.* 2.5-6 and Rom. 7.4-25 is quite instructive. For Paul, the commandment 'You shall not covet' (Rom. 7.7) achieves nothing except to make the human being recognize sin and afford sin the opportunity to come to life in the human being. Paul regards the human as in need of being discharged from the Law in order to produce the fruit of righteousness. For the author of *4 Maccabees*, however, precisely the fact that God gave the commandment 'You shall not covet' (*4 Macc.* 2.5-6) demonstrates that it 'is not too hard for you' (Deut. 30.11). The fruit of the Torah is not awareness of sin and the power of the flesh, but mastery over the passions of the flesh (*4 Macc.* 7.18).

The author of *4 Maccabees* is also considerably more optimistic about the power of the Torah to enable virtuous living than his co-religionist, the author of *4 Ezra*. He laments that, although God gave 'the Law to the descendants of Jacob', yet God

> did not take away their evil heart from them, so that your law might produce fruit in them. For the first Adam, burdened with an evil heart, transgressed and was overcome, as were also all who were descended from him. Thus the disease became permanent; the law was in the hearts of the people along with the evil root; but what was good departed, and the evil remained…(*4 Ezra* 3.12-27; cf. 7.92).

The author of *4 Maccabees* does not speak of an 'evil inclination' within the human being, but merely 'emotions and inclinations' of God's own planting (2.21) over which the mind, strengthened by the Torah, is certainly able to gain mastery.

From the divinely given Law, one comes to know what is 'suitable' for human nature, and what is unsuitable or excessive. For this author, the Law of God is no longer the universal Law of the Stoics standing over against every particular ethnic, human law: it is specifically the Law of Moses, which contains and reveals the universal, absolute Law. Knowledge of the Torah, and strict observance of its instruction, leads to 'wisdom' (1.15-17) and enables the individual to live according to reason, rising above the passions.

The Torah retains, however, its character as covenant. The policies laid out in Deuteronomy 28–30 give the action of the narrative its framework. Indeed, the author's presentation of the historical background to the martyrdoms (3.20–4.26) provides a 'narrative demonstration' (3.19) of the validity of the Deuteronomistic covenant. He begins this narrative, as does his source, 2 Maccabees, with the peace enjoyed under the governance of Onias III, the son of the high priest Simon (praised in Sir. 50.1-23). This enjoyment of peace is the direct result of the people's 'observance of the law', which also brings them recognition and favour from the reigning Seleucid monarch (Seleucus 'Nicanor', 3.20). The story of Simon's treachery and Apollonius's attempt to pillage the Temple treasury proves that divine protection rests upon the Torah-observant Jewish community (3.21-4.14). Simon went to Apollonius, the regional governor, and informed him of rich deposits in the Temple treasury that could lawfully be confiscated for Seleucus the king. Apollonius received Seleucus's authorization to seize the funds in the Temple and proceeded to Jerusalem. He met with the non-violent protests of the Jewish people, who prayed for God's protection of the sanctuary that was about to be desecrated. Apollonius was struck down in his arrogant advance by warrior angels and begged Onias to intercede for him and save his life. Reluctantly, but fearing that Seleucus would suspect foul play rather than divine intervention, Onias agreed and Apollonius returned safely to Seleucus.

Such stories of temple-robbing (a sort of archetypal offence, as in Sophocles, *Oedipus Tyrannus* 884-93) are common to Greek and Jewish narratives. Herodotus (*Persian Wars* 8.35-38) preserved an account of the attempt by the soldiers of Xerxes to take the treasury in the temple at Delphi, a plot that was foiled by natural disaster and supernatural warriors; *3 Macc.* 1.8–2.24 tells a tale in every regard similar to this one, except for the recasting of Ptolemy as the Temple-robber and Eleazar as the high priest. While such stories of miraculous deliverance may meet with the historian's scepticism, they were greeted by the ancients as confirmation of divine justice against the impious and protection for the pious.

The author includes this story because it demonstrates a point of supreme importance: God protects God's sanctuary when the Jewish people are observing the Torah and striving to be faithful to the covenant, affirming that God is able to protect God's honour and the loyal people. Therefore, when disaster strikes, it is not because God is weak (or inferior to the gods of the Gentile conquerors, who are merely agents of God's punishment), but because the covenant has been breached. Both 2 Maccabees and *4 Maccabees* share this basic tenet of Deuteronomistic theodicy.

This story of divine protection of the Temple while the people are faithful provides a juxtaposition to the story of the Hellenization crisis, in which God did not protect God's sanctuary from desecration. The author then introduces Antiochus IV, the antagonist of the narrative. 'Arrogant and terrible', Antiochus represents the 'man of windy pride' whom the Torah (according to Philo, *Virt.* 171), 'sets quite beyond cure, not bringing [him] to be judged by men but handing [him] over to the divine tribunal only, for it says, "Whoever sets his hand to do anything with presumptuousness provokes God"'.

The author provides a strikingly abbreviated account of the Hellenization of Jerusalem and Antiochus's reconquest of the city, desiring not to provide yet another version of the history, but rather just the salient points that touch on his purpose, namely the features that promote loyalty to the Torah and respect for the covenant. When Jason obtains the high priesthood from Antiochus IV by means of a bribe, he

> changed the nation's way of life and altered its form of govern-
> ment in complete violation of the law, so that not only was a
> gymnasium constructed at the very citadel of our native land, but
> also the temple service was abolished. The divine justice was
> angered by these acts and caused Antiochus himself to make war
> on them (4.19-21).

God's patronage and protection of the Jewish people has been symboli-cally and actually rejected by these constitutional modifications—an act that could not be accomplished with impunity.

The oppression that follows appears to be another fulfilment of the curses of Deuteronomy 29 and 30—when the people turn aside from the Torah, God visits them with punishment by means of their ene-mies. The oppression that follows is strikingly reminiscent of Deut.

28.49-50: 'the Lord will bring a nation from far away, from the end of
the earth, to swoop down on you like an eagle…a grim-faced nation
showing no respect to the old or favour to the young'. Later tradition
even speaks of a third 'exile' under Antiochus IV (Schatkin 1974: 99),
reading Deuteronomy's curses more completely into the situation of
167–164 BCE. The inhabitants of Jerusalem were to be punished by the
very people whom they sought to imitate, whose friendship seemed so
desirable in their eyes (cf. 2 Macc. 4.15-17). Such 'poetic justice' is
found also in the meditation in the Wisdom of Solomon on the plagues
sent against Egypt:

> In return for their foolish and wicked thoughts, which led them
> astray to worship irrational serpents and worthless animals, you
> sent upon them a multitude of irrational creatures to punish them,
> so that they might learn that one is punished by the very things by
> which one sins (11.15-16).

Just as God dealt with the Egyptians by punishing them by means of
the symbols of their idolatry, so God dealt with the Israelites who
rejected his covenant in favour of complete Hellenization. The new
relationship with the Seleucid king that seemed so full of promise
became the means by which God chastised God's people for their participation in, or toleration of, Jason's Hellenizing program. In 4.22-26,
God once more uses a Gentile nation as the agent of punishment (as he
had used Nebuchadnezzar).

   The obedience of the martyrs, serving representatively as the return
of the people to the Law (Deut. 30.1-5) and indeed 'reviving observance of the Law' among the Jewish people, brings about a renewal of
the covenant. Again fulfilling the pattern of Deuteronomy, the revival
of obedience turns wrath to mercy, as God once more acts to protect
and preserve God's people (17.22). However, during the Hellenistic
era Deuteronomistic theology was severely challenged, and it was particularly the shameful death of the martyrs that posed the most serious
threat. Did the covenant which, according to the promises of
Deuteronomy, pledged 'long life' and 'length of days' to the righteous
person fail? The Psalms are replete with the expectation that faithful
observance of the Torah would result in vindication, honour and deliverance from disgrace (especially derision by the enemy): 'O that my
ways may be steadfast in keeping your statutes! Then I shall not be put
to shame, having my eyes fixed on all your commandments' (Ps.
119.5-6; cf. Pss. 25.20; 30.2; 70.1; 119.22, 80). For the martyrs, however, obedience to the Torah was specifically the cause of their death in

agony and scorn, while the apostates prospered specifically through their willingness to transgress the ancestral covenant.

During this period, the appeal to reward and punishment beyond death became especially important. The Deuteronomistic promises with regard to the individual did not fail: they were rather postponed to the eternity beyond physical death. The righteous would receive not merely 'long life', but eternal life in God's presence, while the impious would not merely come to an early grave but to everlasting punishment. On Palestinian soil, the hope of the righteous took the form of resurrection. *4 Maccabees*, like Philo and the Wisdom of Solomon (cf. Wis. 3.9), prefer the immaterial 'immortality of the soul': indeed, *4 Maccabees* expunges all references to resurrection contained in his source (cf. 2 Macc. 7.9, 11, 14, 22-23) and replaces this with the more Platonic notion (cf. *4 Macc.* 9.22; 14.5-6; 16.13; 17.12; 18.23). The immortality of the righteous is 'endless life' (17.12), but the immortality of the impious is endless punishment. God remains the zealous defender of God's covenant: those who persecute God's clients will themselves be pursued by divine justice both in the temporal world and throughout eternity (18.22; cf. 9.9; 10.11, 15, 21; 12.12). Similarly, those who transgress the covenant from within expose themselves to eternal danger (13.14-15). Contrary to Redditt's claim (1983: 253-54) that fear of punishment is not a factor in the martyrs' fidelity, the seven brothers certainly do weigh the negative consequences of disobedience: 'Great is the struggle [contest] of the soul and the danger of eternal torment lying before those who transgress the commandment of God' (13.15). The counterpart to not fearing the earthly ruler who commands transgression (13.14) is indeed a healthy fear of the God who commands obedience.

The Torah, then, is both the instructor in virtue—the universal or absolute Law sought by the Hellenistic philosophers as a guide to living 'according to nature'—and the covenant that regulates the relationship between the human clients and the Divine Patron. As was noted in the preceding chapter, the final scriptural citations in the mother's second speech (18.19) leave the audience with two texts framed within Deuteronomistic theology.

Atonement

One of the more striking contributions to Jewish theological reflection is the idea that the 'suffering and death of the martyred righteous had redemptive efficacy for all Israel and secured God's grace and pardon for his people' (Anderson 1985: 539). Two passages especially attest to this way of interpreting the death of the martyrs. First, on the basis of his loyalty to the Law to the point of death, and in the light of the fact that this death is completely voluntary since he could have saved his life through transgression of the Torah, Eleazar prays: 'Be merciful to your people, and let our punishment suffice for them. Make my blood their purification, and take my life in exchange (*antipsuchon*; cf. also 17.21) for theirs' (6.28-29). Secondly, the author looks back upon the achievement of the martyrs in terms of sacrificial language, confirming, as it were, the efficacy of Eleazar's prayer: 'the tyrant was punished, and the homeland purified—they having become, as it were, a ransom for the sin of our nation. And through the blood of those devout ones and their death as an atoning sacrifice, divine Providence preserved Israel that previously had been mistreated' (17.21-22).

This connection of blood and the exchange of a life (*antipsuchos*) recalls the stipulations of LXX Lev. 17.11 for atonement: 'for the life of the flesh is in the blood. This blood I myself have given you to perform the rite of atonement for your lives at the altar; for, as life, it is blood that atones for a life (*anti tēs psuchēs*)'. O'Hagan (1974: 103, 119) is correct to note that the martyr stands as a mediator between the people and God: the martyr becomes a broker, who restores the relationship between the wayward clients and the offended Patron (17.22). Further, the author uses the term *hilastērion* (17.22), which is closely related to the term used in the Septuagint for 'atone', 'propitiate', or 'reconcile' (*exilaskesthai*). Again, the death of the martyrs is the instrument of reconciliation or atonement between God and 'Israel, which previously had been mistreated'. True, this is not a sacrifice prescribed by the Torah, but the obedience that remains steadfast even unto death is accepted by God as (*hōsper*) a sin offering: its effectiveness in achieving atonement, or reconciliation, demonstrates that it is at least the 'dynamic equivalent' of a sin offering.

That the author conceived of the death of Eleazar as an act of expiation may find support in his comparison of Eleazar's bravery in the face of danger with the heroic action of Aaron, who, when a plague had broken out amidst the disobedient wilderness generation, ran into the midst of the people with his censer of incense and made atonement for the people (Num. 16.41-50): 'for just as our father Aaron, armed with the censer, ran through the multitude of the people and conquered the fiery angel, so the descendant of Aaron, Eleazar, though being con-

sumed by the fire, remained unmoved in his reason' (7.11-12). The
precise point of this comparison has eluded scholars, but it cannot be a
feeble point, since the author has even adapted the story of Aaron to
bring it closer into line with Eleazar's ordeal (neither Numbers, nor the
version in Wis. 18.20-25, which already contains advanced angelology,
has any mention of a 'fiery' angel). Both figures are priests; both take a
dangerous stand in order to make atonement for the people and deliver
the nation; both halt the advance of God's agent of wrath by their
bravery. Like Aaron, Eleazar runs into the midst of the wrath as a
champion (cf. Wis. 18.21; here, into the thick of the persecution rather
than the plague), and in the midst of that wrath appeals to God's mercy
and the covenant (cf. Wisd. 18.22b). The comparison with Aaron's act
of expiation, underscores the importance of Eleazar's role in reconciling the people to God.

A number of authors have questioned whether or not the author
truly does posit the atoning efficacy of the martyrs' deaths (S.K.
Williams 1975; Seeley 1990). Seeley (1990: 89-97) wishes to argue that
the 'mimetic process' is more important to the defeat of the tyrant than
the sacrificial aspect of the deaths. He considers this 'the more fundamental, historically conceivable, mode of expressing vicariousness'.
This criterion, however, shows at once his prejudice. A twentieth-cen-
tury scholar may more readily attribute Antiochus's defeat to the
mimetic effect: more and more Israelites followed the example of resistance given in the martyrs. Within the Deuteronomic world-view of
the author, however, God's wrath indeed had to be averted before the
divine punishment could be lifted.

That the death of an individual could atone for the transgression of the
many remains a possible reading of Isa. 52.13–53.12, which to a later
reader might appear to be spoken not by the Gentile nations of Israel but
by sinful Israelites of a particular righteous person within Israel whose
suffering and death are made (by himself, 53.10b, and by God, 53.6b) an
offering for the sins of the collective whole. The Song would be readily
available to the author as a key to the interpretation of Eleazar's death
and that of the mother and her seven sons. The sufferings and mutilations
(Isa. 52.14 and 53.3), the concept of atonement before God through the
willing death of the righteous person (Isa. 53.4-6, 8, 10, 12b), the
affirmation of the efficacy of this unconventional offering (Isa. 53.10b-11)
and the final celebration of the greatness and victory of the suffering servant (Isa. 53.12a) all parallel the case of the Jewish martyrs.

Similarly, LXX Ps. 40.6-8 suggests a radical alteration of the levitical

sacrificial system—one that might have appealed strongly to Diaspora
Jews for whom daily obedience to the Torah and other acts of piety
were more meaningful and accessible than animal sacrifice: 'Sacrifices
and offerings you have not desired, but a body you have prepared for
me; in burnt offerings and sin offerings you have taken no pleasure.
Then I said, "See, God, I have come to do your will" .' The author of
Hebrews (10.5-10) explicitly adduces this text to interpret the death of
another righteous person; it is possible that a similar reading of this text
lies behind the attribution of saving efficacy to the deaths of the righteous heroes of the Antiochene persecution.

The connection of a willing death and the deliverance of a nation is
also well attested in Greek literature, which may provide a supporting
background for the author's interpretation of the martyrs' deaths. The
willingness of the victim was an essential component (Euripides,
Iphigenia at Aulis 1553-56; *Heraclidae* 529-34); the death occurred so
that others might escape death (*Heraclidae*; cf. also Euripides' *Alcestis*)
and so that the country might achieve safety or victory (*Iphigenia at
Aulis*; *Phoenician Women* 997-98; 1013-14). All these aspects are present
in the deaths of the Maccabaean martyrs as well. Eleazar's death on
behalf of the Law becomes a voluntary death (he could have escaped
death, 6.28) offered on behalf of the people, whose sin provoked the
divine justice (4.21).

S.K. Williams (1975: 169) is right, of course, to assert that 'it is not
death *qua* death that is effective but the martyrs' steadfastness, their
endurance, to the point of death itself'. It is not the human blood itself
that atones, but the obedience of these human beings unto death that
God accepts as a perfect sacrifice. In the context of Deuteronomistic
theology, it is obedience (the return to obedience by the people) that
effects reversal of the curses (Deut. 30.1-5). The author has combined
the provisions of Deuteronomy for repentance and renewal of the
covenant blessings (Deut. 30.1-5) with the sacrificial terminology of
Leviticus concerning the sin offering that restores the relationship
between the sinner and God (Lev. 4.1-5.13). Eleazar's 'obedience unto
death' was the act (together with the deaths of the seven brothers and
the mother) that brought reconciliation with God, so that Israel was
preserved (17.22). It is a representative obedience, an obedience maintained on behalf of others (rather than a collective return to obedience
such as Deut. 30.1-5 envisions), so that their deaths readily take on
more of the colouration of a sacrificial act.

This is an important development—one that makes early Christian reflection on the death of Jesus more intelligible (cf. Phil. 2.5-11). S.K. Williams's desire (1975: 176-86) to take the emphasis off the blood and place it on the obedience would have important implications for Christian theology as well (as he is indeed aware): just as the martyrs both reconcile the people to God and revive observance of God's Law, so Jesus' death would be seen under this dual aspect of an act of atonement and a call back to obedience.

While not a sacrifice prescribed by the Torah, the martyrs offer their lives as the only possible sacrifice in a period in which the Temple is defiled and no other sacrifices for sin are feasible. The obedience of the martyrs unto death is indeed viewed by the author as an effective sacrifice—one that God accepts as atonement and that moves God to turn again to God's people in favour and deliverance (cf. van Henten 1993: 123). It is a significant development, for the act of obedience is given the status of sin offering, just as Ps. 141.2 gives cultic significance to acts of piety that are not dependent on a sacrificial system: 'let my prayer be counted as incense before you, and the lifting up of my hands as an evening sacrifice'. Such a development was crucial both to the survival of Judaism after the destruction of the Temple in 70 CE and to the theology of the early Christian movement, for whom the system of animal sacrifices was superseded by the perfect sacrifice of 'obedience unto death'.

Further Reading

Patronage in the Ancient Mediterranean
See 'Further Reading' in Chapter 5.

General Discussions of the Theology of 4 Maccabees
The introductions to the major commentaries include helpful orientations to the theology of *4 Maccabees*, especially Dupont-Sommer (1939: 33-56); Townshend (1913: 653-64); Klauck (1989a: 669-74). Redditt (1983) explores at length the author's development of the concept of the 'law' under the influence mainly of Stoic thought.

Vicarious Atonement in 4 Maccabees
The debate concerning the author's interpretation of the martyrs' deaths as a sacrifice of atonement has been strenuous, largely because of the implications the discussion might have for early Christian interpretation of the death of Jesus (see Chapter 7). S.K. Williams (1975: 169-96) stresses the importance of God's acceptance of the martyrs' endurance as an atoning sacrifice, resisting any temptation to see the martyrs' blood as efficacious *ex opere operato*, and Seeley

(1990: 84-98) builds on the work of Williams to strengthen the case against viewing the martyrs' deaths as atoning sacrifices, but rather as deaths that are 'effective' by means of provoking imitation of their resistance (the 'mimetic process'). In favour of viewing the deaths of martyrs as indeed atoning sacrifices (from the point of view of the author of *4 Maccabees*) are de Jonge (1988; 1991); O'Hagan (1974: 102-19); and van Henten (1993). O'Hagan adduces numerous Jewish parallels in favour of this reading, and de Jonge (1991) identifies the Jewish martyriological conception in which the beneficiary death of martyrs is followed by their post-mortem vindication, to which van Henten adds the important element of the faithfulness (*pistis*) of the martyrs.

Quotations from Seneca have been taken from the LCL edition; quotations from Philo have been taken from the revised edition of Yonge's translation; quotations from the *Letter of Aristeas* have been taken from Hadas (1951).

7

THE INFLUENCE OF *4 MACCABEES*
ON THE EARLY CHURCH

4 Maccabees appears to have enjoyed no lasting influence within post-70 CE Judaism. The retelling of the story of the martyrdom of a mother and her seven sons under the persecution of Hadrian in 135 CE suggests the awareness of 2 Maccabees rather than *4 Maccabees* in rabbinic circles. The story of the martyrdom of the mother with her seven sons did exercise a substantial influence, however, on the piety and thought of the early church. A cult of the martyrs was established in Antioch at a relatively early date: by the time of John Chrysostom it was gaining broad acceptance throughout the Mediterranean. 2 Maccabees was also read and used by the early church. In what follows, I shall attempt to isolate the possible points of contact between *4 Maccabees* specifically and the early church, leaving aside the role of the cult of the martyrs and the influences exercised by the form of the story in 2 Maccabees. We recall from Chapter 1 above that scholars remain uncertain concerning the dating of *4 Maccabees*. The discussion below must therefore remain tentative and suggestive rather than definitive, although even a later date for *4 Maccabees* will still invite investigation into the points of contact between the traditions shared between it and the New Testament texts.

Influence on the New Testament

The most important point of contact and potential influence is the early church's interpretation of the death of Jesus. As the deaths of the martyrs threatened the promises of Deuteronomy, so the scandalous death of Jesus threatened the disconfirmation of the messianic hope. The early Christians, however, began to apply the same language to Jesus' bloody death as the author of *4 Maccabees* had applied to the

bloody death of the martyrs. Jesus' blood takes on a purifying or atoning significance (Rom. 3.25; 5.10; 1 Pet. 1.19; 1 Jn 1.7), in a manner
similar to Eleazar (*4 Macc.* 6.29: 'make my blood their purification').
Jesus was put forward as a 'sacrifice of atonement' or 'propitiation'
(*hilastērion*, Rom. 3.25; cf. *4 Macc.* 17.22). Jesus' death was a death on
behalf of others. Mk 10.45 (= Mt. 20.28) preserves the essence of the
antipsuchos, a 'life in exchange for others' (*4 Macc.* 6.30; 17.22): 'The
Son of Man came...to give his life a ransom for many' (*dounai tēn
psuchēn...anti pollōn*). Elsewhere New Testament authors refer to this
same interpretation with the expressions 'a ransom in exchange' (*anti-
lutron*, 1 Tim. 2.6; compare the related forms in Rom. 3.24; Tit. 2.14;
1 Pet. 1.19) or dying 'on behalf of' others (*huper*, Rom. 5.6, 8; Gal.
2.20; Eph. 5.2; 1 Thess. 5.10; 1 Tim. 2.6; Tit. 2.14), or specifically 'on
behalf of' or 'on account of' the sins of many or all (*huper hamartiōn*, 1
Cor. 15.3; Gal. 1.4; cf. *4 Macc.* 17.21). Significantly, this sacrificial language is not divorced from the recognition that Jesus' obedience, again
like the steadfast obedience of the martyrs (*4 Macc.* 6.27-28), is what is
essential for God's acceptance of his death as an act that brings reconciliation between God and others (Phil. 2.5-11; Rom. 5.19). J.W. van
Henten highlights this aspect of the martyr tradition when he adds the
component of the faithfulness of the martyrs toward God to M. de
Jonge's (1988; 1991) components of a beneficial death followed by
immediate vindication by God (van Henten 1993: 101).

Paul asserts that the claim that Jesus 'died for our sins' is 'in accordance with the Scriptures' (1 Cor. 15.3): Isa. 52.13–53.12 and LXX Ps.
40.6-8 do provide a starting point in the Jewish Scriptures for this
interpretation of the death of Jesus, but *4 Maccabees* has taken an important intermediate step that may well have assisted the early church in
coming to terms with the death of the 'righteous one'. In the words of
S.K. Williams (1975: 253), the author of *4 Maccabees* made 'available to
early Christians, probably in Antioch, a concept in terms of which it
was natural and meaningful for them to interpret the death of another
man faithful unto death, Jesus of Nazareth'. The scope of that reconciliation is, of course, much broader in the case of Jesus. While the obedience unto death of the nine martyrs of *4 Maccabees* makes them a
purification for the nation and an effective atonement reconciling God
and Israel, the early church claims more for the death of Jesus. His obedience unto death (Phil. 2.8) reconciles the world to God, restoring
peace with God for all who have been estranged by sin (2 Cor. 5.14;
Rom. 5.1). Here the ethnic boundaries are broken, and the ideal of

one people under the One God fulfilled (Rom. 3.29-30). Reconcilia
tion between the Divine Patron and the wayward clients, however, is
only part of the achievement in both cases: just as the martyrs' exemplary deaths revived right observance of the Law (*4 Macc.* 18.4), so
Jesus' death paves the way for the fulfilment of God's Law in the reconciled community (Rom. 8.2-4). Even further, just as the martyrs
show the way to conquer the passions of the flesh that hinder obedience to God (18.1-2 and *passim*), so being joined to Jesus provides for
the mastery of the passions of the flesh that are hostile to God's Law
(Gal. 5.16-25; Rom. 8.7-8). The double gift of 'peace' as reconciliation
with God and renewed observance of God's Law links the early
church's understanding of the death of Jesus and *4 Maccabees'* interpretation of the deaths of the martyrs quite closely.

4 Maccabees may also offer insight into one of the voices of the early
church that is not well represented in the New Testament canon,
namely the Torah-observant Gentile mission that strongly rivalled
Paul's mission. If Bickerman's range of dating is essentially correct, and
if we can locate *4 Maccabees* to an urban centre in Syria or Asia Minor,
then this discourse was in a very strong position to exercise some
influence on the growing Christian movement. J.M.G. Barclay (1991)
incisively argues that the Galatian converts were won over by the missionaries of the Torah-observant gospel not merely because of the theological claims made by these rival teachers (reflected in Galatians 3
and 4) but also on account of the ethical guidance that the converts
sought and the rival teachers provided. From Paul's counter-response
to these claims in Gal. 5.1–6.10, we may infer that overcoming the
passions of the flesh was an important element of the rivals' proclamation. Paul must present the better way of mastering the passions (as
living or walking by the Spirit) precisely because a strong case had
been made for following the Torah as the means to this end. Such an
argument for keeping the Torah would have had immediate appeal to
Gentiles, promising the attainment of the virtuous life in language
familiar from Hellenistic ethical philosophy. Such an argument is precisely what one finds in *4 Maccabees*, where the mastery of the 'passions', and even 'the passions of the flesh' (7.18), are a primary topic.
While I would not claim that the Judaizers travelled with a copy of *4
Maccabees* in their baggage, it is certainly worth considering that they
might have been exposed to its argument and used its basic thesis in
their own promotion of Torah-observance to the already converted
Gentiles in Galatia.

A number of scholars have also noted possible lexical and ethical influences of *4 Maccabees* on the Pastoral Epistles (Staples 1966: 220-22). The prominence of 'self-control' (2 Tim. 1.7; Tit. 2.5, 6, 12) and 'piety' (1 Tim. 2.2; 4.7-8; 6.3-6, 11; 2 Tim. 3.5; Titus. 2.12) among the virtues valued in these letters, the awareness of 'desires' or 'passions' (here, *epithumiai*) as the impediment to virtue (2 Tim. 2.22; 3.6; Tit. 2.12; 3.3), as well as the use of the rare word 'incontrovertibly' (*homologoumenōs*, 1 Tim. 3.16), make possible the suggestion that *4 Maccabees* was known to the author(s) of these letters. A loose connection is also apparent in the use of contest imagery. In itself, this sort of metaphor is common enough such that direct dependence need never be suggested. Here, however, the author of the Pastorals speaks of a 'noble contest' (*kalon agōna*), which is specifically a contest of keeping 'faith' (*pistis*) in each use of the image: the encouragement to 'engage the noble contest of faith' (1 Tim. 6.12, my translation) and the testimony to have 'competed in the noble contest…and kept faith' (2 Tim. 4.7, my translation). This recalls rather closely the mother's encouragement to her sons to stand their ground in their 'noble contest' (*4 Macc.* 16.16), having the 'same faith' as Isaac, Daniel and his three companions (16.22).

If *4 Maccabees* was read by the author(s) of the Pastorals, however, it was certainly not read uncritically. 1 Tim. 4.3-5 (cf. Tit. 1.15) specifically contradicts the notion that some foods are proper to eat and some are improper: God created all things, and therefore all things are suitable if received with gratitude. *4 Maccabees* vigorously defends the Jewish food laws, however, attributing to the Torah the role of helping human beings distinguish between suitable and forbidden foods (5.25-26): again, as with Galatians, one may posit a closer connection between *4 Maccabees* and the 'opponents' whose voices are buried within the text of the New Testament.

The author of Hebrews may also have known *4 Maccabees*. Among the examples of faith in Hebrews 11, one finds those who 'were tortured, refusing to accept release, in order to obtain a better resurrection' (11.35b). Scholars frequently refer at this point to 2 Macc. 6.18–7.42, where the story of the martyrdoms of Eleazar and the seven brothers is narrated. Indeed, the expectation of resurrection rather than release for immortality makes 2 Maccabees 7 a more than probable background for Hebrews. The author of Hebrews may also, however, have been familiar with the story as told in *4 Maccabees* 5–18. Hebrews gives the detail that these martyrs did not accept release from their torments, so that they might attain the better resurrection. In 2 Maccabees, the torments of Eleazar and the brothers commence only after they refuse to obey the tyrant. Once begun, they are uninterrupted. In *4 Macc.* 9.16, however, the notion of 'release' from the torments is emphasized: the guards making the offer to the oldest brother, 'Agree to eat so that you may be released from the tortures'. Eleazar is also given a brief respite between tortures in which some members of the king's retinue seek to persuade him to eat and so be released from being tortured to death, an offer which is also refused (6.12-23).

The 'faith' that the addressees of Hebrews are urged to maintain is also similar to the 'faith' that the martyrs are to have (*4 Macc.* 16.22). Just as they are to keep faith with their divine Patron, refusing to dishonour God for the sake of temporary safety or advantage, so the addressees of Hebrews are made aware of their obligations toward the Divine Patron (Heb. 11.6; 12.28) and the eternal dangers of dishonouring God or God's Son (Heb. 6.4-8; 10.26-31) for the sake of relieving the tension that continues to exist between them and the host society. Indeed, the category of 'temporary' advantage is explicitly introduced in Heb. 11.25 (*proskairon*, cf. *4 Macc.* 15.2, 8), and Moses' choice of temporary hardship for the sake of eternal reward (Heb. 11.24-27) parallels very closely the martyrs' similar choice (*4 Macc.* 13.14-17). The addressees of Hebrews are called to maintain this faith and endurance (*hupomonē*, Heb. 12.1) by 'looking to Jesus' (*aphorōntes*, 12.2), just as the martyrs are able by 'looking to God' (*aphorōntes*) to endure 'torture even to death' (*4 Macc.* 17.10).

Several other verses from *4 Maccabees* are echoed in content and form within Hebrews. For example, *4 Macc.* 6.9 speaks thus of Eleazar's posture of endurance: 'he endured the pains and scorned the compulsion' (*hupemene tous ponous kai periephronei tēs anagkēs*, my translation). This bears a striking resemblance to Heb. 12.2, where Jesus, persevering in obedience to God, 'endured a cross, despising shame (*hupemeinen stauron aischunēs kataphronēsas*, my translation). Similarly, *4 Macc.* 17.4, where the author by a literary fiction encourages the mother of the seven martyred brothers to 'take courage...maintaining firm an enduring hope in God' (*tēn elpida tēs hupomonēs bebaian echousa*) bears a certain likeness in thought and vocabulary to Heb. 3.6: 'if we hold firm the confidence and the pride that belong to hope' (*to kauchēma tēs elpidos kataschōmen*); and Heb. 3.14: 'if only we hold our first confidence firm to the end' (*bebaian kataschōmen*). As the martyrs held firm and 'unswerving' (*aklinē*, 17.3), so the addressees of Hebrews are urged to 'hold fast to the confession of our hope [unswervingly]' (*aklinē*, Heb.

10.23). As P. Staples (1966: 221) notes, the benediction of *4 Maccabees* (18.24) and the benedictions of Heb. 13.21 and 2 Tim. 4.18 are strikingly similar.

J.W. van Henten has argued strongly for greater care in positing literary dependence between Christian and Jewish martyrological texts (1995: 309-10). The use of athletic metaphors or the notion of endurance 'unto death' are rightly described as being too general to establish the use of one text by another author. He suggests a minimum of three verbal parallels within one coherent passage of both texts as evidence of such use. The use of *4 Maccabees* by Hebrews comes very close to meeting this criterion, and, if one were to allow some liberty with regard to the definition of 'one coherent passage', these verbal parallels would provide a strong case indeed for literary dependance between Hebrews and *4 Maccabees*.

As a final point of contact, one may note that the ideology of martyrdom in *4 Maccabees* bears some resemblances to that of the Apocalypse of John, as to early Christian martyriology more generally (see next section). Both books are concerned with bearing 'witness' or preserving a 'testimony', and in both books this task involves suffering and death (Rev. 6.9; 11.3-12; 12.11). Thus Jesus and Antipas are both 'faithful witnesses' (Rev. 1.5; 2.13), and the criterion of honour and reward is holding firm 'the testimony of Jesus' (1.9; 12.17). The martyrs of both texts lay down their lives for the sake of being faithful witnesses to the message of God. In both texts, conquering the enemy (defeating the tyrant) occurs by dying (Rev. 2.7, 11, 17, 26; 3.5, 12, 21; 12.11; 15.2; cf. *4 Macc.* 1.1; 6.10; 7.4; 9.30; 11.20). The martyrs of *4 Maccabees* and of Revelation overcome by not yielding to the pressures of the dominant culture to accommodate, sacrificing the exclusive loyalty called for by the One God of Judaeo-Christian confession. Endurance (*hupomonē*) is, therefore, a virtue prized in both texts (Rev. 1.9; 2.2, 3, 19; 13.10; *4 Macc.* 1.11; 7.9; 9.8, 30; 15.30; 17.4, 12, 17, 23). Finally, the death of the martyr is not a degradation, but rather the path to eternal honour: both texts speak of crowning as the honourable prize of dying for the sake of piety (Rev. 2.10; *4 Macc.* 17.15), as well as the martyrs standing 'before the throne of God' (Rev. 7.15; *4 Macc.* 17.18).

I have spoken above of 'points of contact' between *4 Maccabees* and the New Testament. It is less important to force the issue of direct dependence (although there are cases where correspondences are sufficiently numerous to make a plausible case), than to recognize that

4 Maccabees provides a very useful window both into the convictions of groups within early Christianity that have been silenced by history as well as insights into the convictions of the canonical texts themselves. The uncertainty about the date of the composition of *4 Maccabees* also must lead one to caution in considering direct influence, although from a tradition-historical standpoint it is simpler to account for the wide-spread points of contact through positing familiarity with *4 Maccabees* on the part of numerous early Christian authors. *4 Maccabees* represents an important intermediate step between the identification of Jesus' death as a saving event and the 'Scriptures' that support such a reading (cf. 1 Cor. 15.3). It provides the sort of argumentation that Gentile converts to a Torah-free Christianity might have found persuasive on the lips of missionaries of a Torah-observant gospel. It shares with the Pastorals an endeavour to present the religious faith of a minority group as a respectable option within the dominant culture. It shares with Hebrews and Revelation the elevation of loyalty to the Divine Patron above any temporal disadvantages incurred by such a stance, making endurance of suffering, disadvantage and even death the path to reward, advantage, and honour. While there are significant differences between the actual purpose of *4 Maccabees* (promotion of strict Torah observance) and the New Testament texts, the linguistic, ethical, social and theological points of contact between them make *4 Maccabees* a potentially important influence on the early Christian movement.

right area to hear/read 4 Mac.

Influence on Early Christian Martyriology

The ideology of the martyr encountered in *4 Maccabees* appears to have exercised a strong influence on the thinking of Ignatius, bishop of Antioch, as he went to his own martyrdom in or near 110 CE. As W. Frend (1967: 152) notes, 'like the Maccabees in the tradition of the *under?* Antiochene–Jewish *4 Maccabees* he regards his death in sacrificial terms, and as "sweet" and as a "grace" '. The second brother had called his martyrdom 'sweet' (*4 Macc. 9.29*), and the fifth referred to the opportunities for martyrdom as 'splendid favours' (= 'grace', *4 Macc. 11.12*). Similarly, just as *4 Maccabees* uses the term *antipsuchos* (6.29; 17.21) to describe the beneficial effects of the martyrs' deaths for the nation, so Ignatius uses this term four times in the same sense of an atoning sacrifice in place of' others: 'May my soul be given for yours, and for them whom you sent in the honour of God to Smyrna' (Ignatius, *Eph.* 21.1); 'May my spirit be in substitution for your life' (Ignatius, *Smyrn.*

Ignatius, Mart. Poly., Martyrs of Lyons

10.2; cf. also Ignatius, *Pol.* 2.3; 6.1). It is more likely that Ignatius borrowed this terminology from martyr ideology rather than from Christology. Ignatius invites the commencement of his trial in a manner highly reminiscent of Eleazar: 'Come fire and cross and grapplings with wild beasts, wrenching of bones, hacking of limbs, crushings of my whole body, come cruel tortures of the devil to assail me' (Ignatius, *Rom.* 5.3; cf. *4 Macc.* 5.32). Finally, the result of martyrdom is described in both texts as a 'rebirth' or 'new birth' (*4 Macc.* 16.13; cf. Ignatius, *Rom.* 6.1), and the sufferings themselves are compared with 'birth pangs' (*4 Macc.* 15.16; Ignatius, *Rom.* 6.1: 'The pangs of a new birth are upon me'). Van Henten (1986: 137) adds a number of useful observations concerning points of contact between the two martyr ideologies. Ignatius sees martyrdom as the fulfilment of his earthly life, and sets a lower value on 'this age'. He shares with the martyrs of *4 Maccabees* the idea that only through martyrdom can they validate their existence as Jews or Christians (Ignatius, *Rom.* 6.2; *4 Macc.* 5.34-35; 7.9). Martyrdom makes Ignatius's faith reality, not mere reputation (Ignatius, *Rom.* 3.2; *4 Macc.* 5.18; 6.18). These close verbal and conceptual parallels, together with the possibility that *4 Maccabees* was written in Antioch (or at least in a neighbouring region), the city that certainly at least kept the tradition of the nine martyrs alive, lends support here to a hypothesis of direct influence.

The mid-second-century document *Martyrdom of Polycarp* also carries traces of awareness of the portrayal of the martyrdoms in *4 Maccabees*. Before the execution is carried out, Polycarp is given a chance to offer incense to the emperor. The proconsul's invitation is very similar to Antiochus's invitation to Eleazar (*4 Macc.* 5.11-12): 'the proconsul tried to persuade him to a denial saying, "Have respect for thine age"', and other things in accordance therewith, as it is their wont to say' (*Mart. Pol.* 9). The final phrase provides evidence that the antagonist's portrayal in martyriologies has already become somewhat conventionalized, and *4 Maccabees* is the earliest expression of this particular convention (hence perhaps its originator). Polycarp's refusal is framed with the same logic found in the seven brothers, who prefer to face the torments that last for a season rather than procure temporary safety at the cost of eternal punishment, the fate of the impious (*4 Macc.* 9.7-9, 31-32; 10.11; 13.14-15): 'you threaten that fire which burns for a season and after a little while is quenched: for you are ignorant of the fire of the future judgement and eternal punishment, which is reserved for the ungodly' (*Mart. Pol.* 11). The *Martyrdom of Polycarp* (1; 13; 17) continues the sense given to the word 'witness' found in *4 Macc.* 16.16 as a testimony given through the endurance of sufferings and death. The death of the martyr is again a new birth (*Mart. Pol.* 18; cf. *4 Macc.* 16.13); the martyr carries off the prize (*Mart. Pol.* 17; cf. *4 Macc.* 16.28; 17.12) and the reward of his testimony is a 'crown of immortality' (*Mart. Pol.* 17, 20; cf. *4 Macc.* 17.12, 15). Once more, there are enough points of correspondence to suggest that *4 Maccabees* was formative at some level for the shaping of the account of Polycarp's martyrdom.

W. Frend (1967: 19) also draws attention to the similarities between the epistolary account of the martyrs of Lyons (preserved in Eusebius, *History* 5.1.1-61) and *4 Maccabees*. Both texts make extensive use of the 'contest' metaphor to describe the martyrdoms, and in both the martyrs are explicitly called 'athletes'. The figure of Blandina, however, seems to be especially patterned after the figure of the mother:

> To crown all this, on the last day of the sports Blandina was again brought in, and with her Ponticus, a lad of about fifteen. Day after day they had been taken in to watch the rest being punished, and attempts were made to make them swear by the heathen idols. When they stood firm and treated these efforts with contempt, the mob was infuriated with them, so that the boy's tender age called forth no pity and the woman no respect. They subjected them to every horror and inflicted every punishment in turn, attempting again and again to make them swear, but to no purpose. Ponticus was encouraged by his sister in Christ, so that the heathen saw that she was urging him on and stiffening his resistance, and he bravely endured every punishment until he gave back his spirit to God. Last of all, like a noble mother who had encouraged her children and sent them before her in triumph to the King, blessed Blandina herself passed through all the ordeals of her children and hastened to rejoin them, rejoicing and exulting at her departure as if invited to a wedding supper, not thrown to the beasts (*History* 5.1.53-55).

Encouraging the young to endure for the sake of God is a role shared by Blandina and the mother in *4 Maccabees*, and indeed the simile used to describe Blandina makes this connection explicit. While in itself this episode may recall either 2 Maccabees or *4 Maccabees*, the use of athletic imagery in the same document suggests rather the latter as the primary inspiration. In Ignatius's own reflections on his martyrdom and in the accounts of the deaths of Polycarp and the martyrs of Lyons, the traces of the influence of *4 Maccabees* are rather strong. Even though the latter text urged commitment to the Torah for the sake of God, it nevertheless provided a useful vocabulary for speaking of the noble death suffered on account of piety, the deliberations that supported such a choice, and the rewards of those who valued God's favour more than this present life.

Influence on the Church Fathers

During the third century, persecution of Christians had increased. Origen wrote an *Exhortation to Martyrdom* to two deacons in Caesarea during the persecution of Christian clergy by Maximin in 235 CE and following, using the story of Eleazar, the mother and the seven brothers to encourage these young men to face the last extremity of devotion. Winslow (1974: 81) claims that Origen is using 2 Maccabees, and Rowan Greer even introduces into his translation of this text the further specification of Origen's citation of his source ('written in the Maccabees') as 2 Maccabees. There are significant connections with *4 Maccabees*, however, and enough resonances with details in *4 Maccabees* not found in 2 Maccabees to suggest that Origen also knew the story as it was rendered in *4 Maccabees*.

Origen's *Exhortation* frequently appeals to the metaphor of the athletic 'contest' when speaking of the Christian's trial and martyrdom. Origen cites several New Testament Scriptures that combine the *agōn* motif and death in such a way as to be fruitful for interpreting martyrdom as a contest (2 Tim. 4.7-8; Heb. 12.1-4). Many of his precise applications of this metaphor, however, derive from *4 Maccabees* rather than the New Testament. First, the New Testament does not use the word 'athlete' (*athlētēs*), which is consistently Origen's term for the Christian competing for the prize of faithfulness. Origen even uses the compound 'noble athlete' (*gennaios athlētēs*, 1.11, 23.23), a compound formulated by the author of *4 Maccabees* (6.10). Similarly, Origen calls these brothers 'devotees for piety' (23.23, 27-28), a title not used in 2 Maccabees but present exactly in this form in *4 Macc.* 12.11 ('those who practice religion'), and related to *4 Maccabees*' assertions that the martyrs die 'for the sake of religion' (5.31; 6.22; 9.30; 11.20; 13.12). Origen also describes the martyrs as 'those competing for virtues', an echo of *4 Macc.* 12.14 (the 'contestants for virtue'), as well as the frequent mention in *4 Maccabees* of the fact that they die for the sake of virtue (*aretē* or *kalokagathia*: 1.8; 9.8; 13.25, etc). It is *4 Maccabees*, not 2 Maccabees that explicitly and frequently likens the martyrdoms to a contest (cf. 16.16-17; 17.11-16), and this tendency strongly colours Origen's retelling of the martyrdoms.

Other details in Origen's *Exhortation* point to *4 Maccabees*' influence.

Origen observes that Antiochus's forcing the brothers to watch each other's death was part of the ordeal—an observation explicitly made by *4 Macc.* 13.27, but left unspoken in 2 Maccabees. Origen advises early in his discourse (*Exhortation* 4) that one should not turn one's eyes away from God to show fear of those who will themselves die and be subject to God's judgment, which is exactly the advice shared among the brothers in *4 Macc.* 13.14-15. While Origen may have derived this from Mt. 10.28, *4 Maccabees* had already presented this contrast in the context of eternal reward and punishment—it had taken an intermediate step between Mt. 10.28 and Origen. Moreover, *Exhortation* 28 draws an inference highly reminiscent of *4 Macc.* 16.18-19 and 13.13: 'Since a saint is generous and wishes to respond to the benefits that have overtaken him from God, he searches out what he can do for the Lord in return for everything he has obtained from Him. And he finds that nothing else can be given to God from a person of high purpose that will so balance His benefits as perfection in martyrdom.' Origen's depiction of giving one's life for God through martyrdom as a just exchange for the life received from God is already formulated in *4 Macc.* 13.13 and 16.18-19. Just as *4 Maccabees*, then, strengthened the Christian martyrs of the second century and influenced the portrayal of their sufferings, so it continued to be useful into the third century for the same purpose of moral exhortation.

4 Maccabees continued to enjoy popularity among Christians even after the threat of official persecution (for the members of the Great Church) was virtually eliminated by Constantine's conversion and decrees. Sermons of both Gregory of Nazianzen and John Chrysostom have been preserved praising these martyrs and recommending their example to the congregation. The former leaves no doubt that he has read *4 Maccabees*, referring in his oration to 'the Book which philosophizes about Reason being supreme over the passions'. Both authors recognized the anomaly of revering pre-Christian saints, and indeed the tendency of many Christians to disregard the observance of their festival precisely for this cause: 'What of the Maccabaeans? For today is their anniversary; though by many they be not honoured because their contest (*athlēsis*) was not after Christ, yet they are worthy to be honoured by all, in that their endurance was in behalf of the Law of their fathers' (Gregory of Nazianzen, *Oration 15,* as quoted in Townshend 1913: 658). John Chrysostom even argues that their achievement is even greater than that of Christian martyrs, 'because they fought before the brazen gates of the kingdom of Satan were destroyed, when even

the just like Moses feared death' (*Homilia de Eleazaro et septem filiis 2*,
PG 63.525-26, as quoted in Schatkin 1974: 113).

The influence of 4 Maccabees on Christian moral exhortation out-
lasted the persecution of the church, and the martyrs remained vivid
examples of obedience to God and endurance of any deprivation for
the sake of piety. The battle of the martyrs against Antiochus was transferred to the spiritual battle between the soul and its eternal adversary,
ever seeking to seduce it into indulging sinful passions and abandoning
the noble contest for virtue, or to the battle between the orthodox and
heterodox Christians. Interest in *4 Maccabees* as an exhortation to martyrdom on behalf of witness to the truth came into vogue once more,
when Erasmus offered a paraphrase of the work, of special interest to
him because the possibility of martyrdom was renewed during the
Reformation and its aftermath, and Erasmus's own works came once
under the scrutiny of the Inquisition. It remains an enduring witness to
the dignity of the human being, who is reminded by its testimony that
he or she need never submit to any external or internal compulsion
that compromises his or her self respect.

Further Reading

Vicarious Atonement in 4 Maccabees *and early Christian Soteriology*
The view that the martyrology of 2 Maccabees and *4 Maccabees* is an important
development between Isaiah's Suffering Servant and early Christian interpretation of the death of Jesus is perhaps best represented in de Jonge (1991). See
also the works listed under 'Vicarious Atonement in *4 Maccabees*' at the end of
Chapter 6.

Influence of 4 Maccabees *on Early Christianity*
Staples (1966) discusses points of contact between the Pastoral Epistles and *4
Maccabees*, noting especially the similarity of the benedictions, and presses
beyond these observations to the speculative hypothesis that Alexandrian
Christianity had direct connections with churches in Asia Minor and introduced *4 Maccabees* to those assemblies. Van Henten (1993) compares the presentation of the martyrs with the interpretation of Jesus' death in Romans 3.25,
regarding the lexical similarities as especially important evidence of an underly-
ing, common tradition.

Frend (1967) provides the classic survey of persecution in the Hellenistic and
Roman periods and the development of Christian martyrology. On the
influence of *4 Maccabees* on early Christian martyr stories, see Perler (1949),
who argues for the direct influence of *4 Maccabees* upon Ignatius and Martyrdom of Polycarp. A useful caution is offered by van Henten (1995), who

reflects methodologically on how the similarities between Jewish and Christian
martyr stories should be evaluated, pointing to the function of the martyrs
within each group as heroes of a special 'nation' and as models of endurance.
Townshend (1913: 653-64) contains a valuable survey of the use of *4 Maccabees*
by Ante-Nicene and Post-Nicene Fathers. Winslow (1974) traces the use of
the martyr stories specifically in Cyprian, Origen, Augustine and Gregory.

A number of articles have attempted to locate the actual cite of the martyrdoms that form the basis for *4 Maccabees* and 2 Maccabees 6–7. Obermann
(1931) argues that the martyrdoms occurred in Jerusalem, not Antioch.
Schatkin (1974) attempts to demonstrate, against Obermann, that the martyrdoms took place in Antioch. This second article is more valuable for its compi-
lation of patristic references to these martyrs.

Quotations from Ignatius and the *Martyrdom of Polycarp* have been taken from
Staniforth (1968); quotations from Eusebius have been taken from the translation by Williamson in the Penguin edition; quotations from Origen have been
taken from the translation by Greer in the Paulist Press edition; quotations
from Gregory of Nazianzen have been taken from Townshend (1913); quotations from Chrysostom have been taken from Schatkin (1974).

Bibliography

Primary Sources

Aeschylus (trans. H.W. Smyth; LCL; 2 vols.; London: Heinemann; Cambridge, MA: Harvard University Press, 1922, 1926).

The Apostolic Fathers (trans. Kirsopp Lake; LCL; 2 vols.; London: Heinemann; Cambridge, MA: Harvard University Press, 1912, 1913).

Aristeas, *Letter of Aristeas to Philocrates* (see Hadas 1951).

Aristotle, *The Art of Rhetoric* (trans. J.H. Freese; LCL; London: Heinemann; Cambridge, MA: Harvard University Press, 1926).

Aristotle, *Athenian Constitution, Eudemian Ethics, Virtues and Vices* (trans. H. Rackham; LCL; London: Heinemann: Cambridge, MA: Harvard University Press, 1935).

Aristotle, *Nicomachean Ethics* (trans. H. Rackham; LCL; London: Heinemann; Cambridge, MA: Harvard University Press, 1926).

Aristotle, *Poetics* (trans. S. Halliwell; LCL; London: Heinemann; Cambridge, MA: Harvard University Press, 1927).

Aristotle, *Politics* (trans. H. Rackham; LCL; London: Heinemann; Cambridge, MA: Harvard University Press, 1932).

Aristotle, *Rhetorica ad Alexandrum* (trans. H. Rackham; LCL; London: Heinemann; Cambridge, MA: Harvard University Press, 1957).

Cicero, *De Oratore Book III, De Fato, Paradoxa Stoicorum, De Partitione Oratoria* (trans. H. Rackham; LCL; London: Heineman; Cambridge, MA: Harvard University Press, 1942).

Cicero, *Rhetorica ad Herennium* (trans. H. Caplan; LCL; London: Heinemann; Cambridge, MA: Harvard University Press, 1954).

Cicero, *Tusculun Disputations* (trans. J.E. King; LCL; London: Heinemann; Cambridge, MA: Harvard University Press, 1927).

Demosthenes, *Funeral Speech (LX), Erotic Assay (LXI), Exordia, Letters* (trans. N.W. De Witt and N.J. De Witt; LCL; London: Heinemann; Cambridge, MA: Harvard University Press, 1949).

Dio Chrysostom, *Orations* (trans. J.W. Cohoon and H.L. Crosby; LCL; 5 vols.; London: Heinemann; Cambridge, MA: Harvard University Press, 1932–51).

Diodorus of Sicily, *Library of History* (various translators; LCL; 12 vols.; London: Heinemann; Cambridge, MA: Harvard University Press, 1933–67).

Diogenes Laertius, *Lives of Eminent Philosophers* (trans. R.D. Hicks; LCL; 2 vols.; London: Heinemann; Cambridge, MA: Harvard University Press, 1925).

Dionysius of Halicarnassus, *The Roman Antiquities of Dionysius of Halicarnassus* (trans. Earnest Cary; LCL; 7 vols.; London: Heinemann; Cambridge, MA: Harvard University Press, 1937–50).

Epictetus, *The Discourses as Reported by Arrian, the Manual, and Fragments* (trans. W. A.

Oldfather; LCL; 2 vols.; London: Heinemann; Cambridge, MA: Harvard University Press, 1925, 1928).

Euripides, *Tragedies* (trans. A.S. Way; LCL; 4 vols.; London: Heinemann; Cambridge, MA: Harvard University Press, 1912).

Eusebius, *The History of the Church* (trans. G.A. Williamson; London: Penguin Books, 1965).

Herodotus, *The Persian Wars* (trans. A.D. Godley; LCL; 4 vols.; London: Heinemann; Cambridge, MA: Harvard University Press, 1920–24).

Horace, *Satires, Epistles, Ars Poetica* (trans. H.R. Fairclough; LCL; London: Heinemann; Cambridge, MA: Harvard University Press, 1926).

Josephus, *The Jewish War* (trans. H. St. John Thackeray; LCL; 2 vols.; London: Heinemann; Cambridge, MA: Harvard University Press, 1927, 1928).

Josephus, *The Life, Against Apion* (trans. H. St. John Thackeray; LCL: London: Heinemann; Cambridge, MA: Harvard University Press, 1926).

Josephus, *Jewish Antiquities* (trans. H. St. John Thackeray, Ralph Marcus and Allen Wikgren; LCL; 5 vols.; London: Heinemann; Cambridge, MA: Harvard University Press, 1930, 1963).

Josephus, *The Works of Josephus* (trans. W. Whiston; Peabody, MA: Hendrickson, 1987).

Juvenal, *Satires*, in *Juvenal and Persius* (trans. G.G. Ramsey: LCL; London Heinemann; Cambridge, MA: Harvard University Press, 1928).

Lucian, *The Downward Journey, or the Tyrant* and *The Tyrannicide* in *Works* I, V (trans. A. M. Harmon; LCL; 8 vols.; London: Heinemann; Cambridge, MA: Harvard University Press, 1913–67).

Lysias, *Orations* (trans. W.R.M. Lamb; LCL; London: Heinemann; Cambridge, MA: Harvard University Press, 1930).

Origen, *An Exhortation to Martyrdom* (trans. R.A. Greer *et al.*; New York: Paulist Press, 1979).

Philo, *Works* (trans. F.H. Colson, G.H. Whitaker and Ralph Marcus; LCL; 12 vols.; London: Heinemann; Cambridge, MA: Harvard University Press, 1929–53).

Philo, *The Works of Philo* (trans. C. D. Yonge; Peabody, MA: Hendrickson, 1993).

Plato, *The Dialogues of Plato* (trans. Benjamin Jowett [with 'The Seventh Letter'; trans. J. Harvard]; Chicago: William Benton, 1952).

Plato, *Euthyphro, Apology, Crito, Phaedo, Phaedrus* (trans. H.N. Fowler; LCL; London: Heinemann; Cambridge, MA: Harvard University Press, 1914).

Plato, *Laches, Protagoras, Meno, Euthydemus* (trans. W.R.M. Lamb; LCL; London: Heinemann: Cambridge, MA: Harvard University Press, 1924).

Plato, *Lysis, Symposium, Gorgias* (trans. W.R.M. Lamb; LCL; London: Heinemann; Cambridge, MA: Harvard University Press, 1925).

Plato, *The Republic [Respublica]* (trans. P. Shorey; LCL; 2 vols.; London: Heinemann; Cambridge, MA: Harvard University Press, 1930, 1935).

Pliny the Younger, *Letters and Panegyricus* (trans. B. Radice; LCL; 2 vols.; London: Heinemann; Cambridge, MA: Harvard University Press, 1969).

Plutarch, *Moralia* (various translators; LCL; 15 vols.; London: Heinemann; Cambridge, MA: Harvard University Press, 1927–76).

Quintilian, *Institutio Oratoria* (trans. H.E. Butler; LCL; London: Heinemann; Cambridge, MA: Harvard University Press, 1921).

Seneca, *Ad Lucilium Epistulae Morales* (trans. R.M. Gummere; LCL; 3 vols.; London: Heinemann; Cambridge, MA: Harvard University Press, 1917–25).

Seneca, *De beneficiis, De constantia, De ira, De providentia*, in *Moral Essays* (trans, J.W.

Basore; LCL; 3 vols.; London: Heinemann; Cambridge, MA: Harvard University Press, 1928–35).

Seneca, *Hercules Furens*, in *Tragedies* (trans. F.J. Miller; LCL; 2 vols.; London: Heinemann; Cambridge, MA: Harvard University Press, 1917).

Seneca, *Moral Essays* (trans. J.W. Basore; LCL; 3 vols.; London: Heinemann; Cambridge, MA: Harvard University Press, 1928–35).

Sophocles, *Tragedies* (trans. Hugh Lloyd-Jones; LCL; 3 vols.; London: Heinemann; Cambridge, MA: Harvard University Press, 1994–96).

Stoicorum veterum fragmenta (ed. J. von Arnim; 4 vols.; Leipzig, 1903–24)

Suetonius, *The Twelve Caesars* (trans. J.H. Rolfe; LCL; 2 vols.; London: Heinemann; Cambridge, MA: Harvard University Press, 1914).

Suetonius, *Vespasian*, in *The Twelve Caesers* (trans. J.H. Rolfe; LCL; 2 vols.; London: Heinemann; Cambridge, MA: Harvard University Press, 1914).

Tacitus, *The Agricola and the Germania* (trans. H. Mattingly; London: Penguin Books, 1948).

Tacitus, *The Histories* (trans. K. Wellesley; London: Penguin Books, 1964).

Thucydides, *Histories* (trans. C.F. Smith; LCL; 4 vols.; London: Heinemann; Cambridge, MA: Harvard University Press, 1919–23).

Xenophon, *Cyropaedia* (trans. W. Miller; LCL; 2 vols.; London: Heinemann; Cambridge, MA: Harvard University Press, 1914).

Xenophon, *Memorabilia and Oeconomicus* (trans. E.C. Marchant; LCL; London: Heinemann; Cambridge, MA: Harvard University Press, 1923).

Secondary Sources

Amir, Y.
    1971   'Maccabees, Fourth Book of', *Enc Jud*, XI: 661-62.
Anderson, H.
    1985   '4 Maccabees (First Century AD): A New Translation and Introduction', *OTP* II: 531-64.
    1992   'Maccabees, Books of: Fourth Maccabees', *ABD* IV: 452-43.
Aune, D.C.
    1994   'Mastery of the Passions: Philo, 4 Maccabees and Earliest Christianity', in Wendy Helleman (ed.), *Hellenization Revisited: Shaping a Christian Response within the Greco-Roman World* (Lanham, MD: University Press of America): 125-58.
Barclay, J.M.G.
    1991   *Obeying the Truth* (Minneapolis: Fortress Press).
Bickerman, E.J.
    1976a   'The Date of Fourth Maccabees', in E.J. Bickerman, *Studies in Jewish and Christian History* (Leiden: E. J. Brill): I, 275-81.
    1976b   'The Maccabean Uprising: An Interpretation', in Judah Goldin (ed.), *The Jewish Expression* (New Haven: Yale University Press): 66-86.
    1979   *The God of the Maccabees: Studies on the Meaning and Origin of the Maccabean Revolt* (SJLA; Leiden: E.J. Brill).
Boissevain, J.
    1974   *Friends of Friends: Networks, Manipulators and Coalitions* (New York: St. Martin's).

Breitenstein, U.
1978   *Beobachtungen zu Sprache: Stil und Gedankengut des Vierten Makkabäerbuchs* (Basel/Stuttgart: Schwabe).

Butts, J.R.
1986   'The Progymnasmata of Theon: A New Text with Translation and Commentary' (PhD Dissertation, Claremont Graduate School).

Collins, J.J.
1983   *Between Athens and Jerusalem* (New York: Crossroad).

Crossan, J.D.
1991   *The Historical Jesus: The Life of a Mediterranean Jewish Peasant* (San Francisco: HarperCollins).

Danby, H.
1933   *The Mishnah, Translated from the Hebrew with Introduction and Brief Explanatory Notes* (Oxford: Oxford University Press).

Danker, F.W.
1982   *Benefactor: Epigraphic Study of a Graeco-Roman and New Testament Semantic Field* (St.. Louis, MO: Clayton Publishing House).

Deissmann, A.
1900   'Das vierte Makkabäerbuch', in E. Kautzsch (ed.), *Die Apokryphen und Pseudepigraphen des Alten Testaments* (Hildesheim: Georg Olms) II: 149-76.

deSilva, D.A.
1995a   *Despising Shame: Honor Discourse and Community Maintenance in the Epistle to the Hebrews* (SBLDS, 152; Atlanta: Scholars Press).
1995b   'The Noble Contest: Honor, Shame, and the Rhetorical Strategy of *4 Maccabees*', *JSP* 13: 31-57.
1996a   'Exchanging Favor for Wrath: Apostasy in Hebrews and Patron-Client Relations', *JBL* 115: 91-116.
1996b   'The Wisdom of Ben Sira: Honor, Shame, and the Maintenance of the Values of a Minority Culture', *CBQ* 58: 433-55.

Droge, A.J., and J.D. Tabor.
1992   *A Noble Death: Suicide and Martyrdom among Christians and Jews in Antiquity* (San Francisco: HarperSanFrancisco).

Dupont-Sommer, A.
1939   *Le Quatrième Livre des Machabées* (Paris: Librairie Ancienne Honoré Champion).

Frend, W.H.C.
1967   *Martyrdom and Persecution in the Early Church: A Study of Conflict from the Maccabees to Donatus* (New York: New York University Press).

Freudenthal, J.
1869   *Die Flavius Josephus beigelegte Schrift über die Herrschaft der Vernunft (IV Makkabäerbuch): Eine Predigt aus dem ersten nachchristlichen Jahrhundert* (Breslau).

Gager, J.
1983   *The Origins of Anti-Semitism: Attitudes Toward Judaism in Pagan and Christian Antiquity* (Oxford: Oxford University Press).

Gilbert, M.
1984   '4 Maccabees', in M.E. Stone (ed.), *Jewish Writings of the Second Temple Period* (Assen: Van Gorcum; Philadelphia: Fortress Press): 316-19.

Goldstein, J.
1976   *I Maccabees: A New Translation with Introduction and Commentary* (AB, 41; Garden City, NY: Doubleday).
1983   *II Maccabees: A New Translation with Introduction and Commentary* (AB, 41A; Garden City, NY: Doubleday).

Grimm, C.L.W.
1857   'Viertes Buch der Maccabäer', in *Kunzgefasstes exegetisches Handbuch zu den Apokryphen des Alten Testaments* (Leipzig): 283-370.

Hadas, M.
1951   *Aristeas to Philocrates* (New York: Harper & Brothers).
1953   *The Third and Fourth Books of Maccabees* (New York: Harper & Brothers).

Harrington, D.J.
1988   *The Maccabean Revolt: Anatomy of a Biblical Revolution* (Wilmington, DE: Michael Glazier).

Heininger, B.
1989   'Der böse Antiochus: Eine Studie zur Erzähltechnik des 4. Makkabäerbuchs', *BZ* NS 33: 43-59.

Hengel, M.
1974   *Judaism and Hellenism* (2 vols.; Philadelphia: Fortress Press).
1980   *Jews, Greeks, and Barbarians: Aspects of the Hellenization of Judaism in the Pre-Christian Period* (Philadelphia: Fortress Press).

Hock, R.F., and E.N. O'Neil
1986   *The Chreia in Ancient Rhetoric.* I. *The Progymnasmata* (Atlanta: Scholars Press).

de Jonge, M.
1988   'Jesus' Death for Others and the Death of the Maccabean Martyrs', in T. Baarda *et al.* (eds.), *Text and Testimony: Essays on New Testament and Apocryphal Literature in Honor of A.J.F. Klijn* (Kampen: Kok) 142-51.
1991   *Jesus, the Servant Messiah* (New Haven: Yale University Press).

Johnson, S.E., and John Breck.
1991   '4 Maccabees', in B.M. Metzger and R.E. Murphy (eds.), *The New Oxford Annotated Bible: New Revised Standard Version* (New York: Oxford University Press).

Kennedy, G.A.
1984   *New Testament Interpretation through Rhetorical Criticism* (Chapel Hill: University of North Carolina Press).

Klauck, H.-J.
1989a *4 Makkabäerbuch* (JSHRZ, 3.6.; Gütersloh: Gerd Mohn).
1989b 'Hellenistiche Rhetorik im Diasporajudentum: Das Exordium des vierten Makkabäerbuchs (4 Makk 1.1-12), *NTS* 35: 451-65.
1990   'Brotherly Love in Plutarch and in 4 Maccabees', in D.L. Balch, E. Ferguson, and W.A. Meeks (eds.), *Greeks, Romans, Christians* (Minneapolis: Fortress Press): 144-56.

Lauer, S.
1955   '*Eusebes Logismos* in IV Macc', *JJS* 6: 170-71.

Lebram, J.C.H.
1974   'Die literarische Form des vierten Makkabäerbuches', *VC* 28: 81-96.

Mack, B.L.
1990   *Rhetoric and the New Testament* (Minneapolis: Augsburg–Fortress).

Mack, B.L., and V.K. Robbins
    1989   *Patterns of Persuasion in the Gospels* (Sonoma, CA: Polebridge Press).
Malina, B.J., and J.H. Neyrey
    1991   'Conflict in Luke–Acts: Labelling and Deviance Theory', in J. H. Neyrey
            (ed.), *The Social World of Luke–Acts: Models for Interpretation* (Peabody, MA:
            Hendrickson).
Marrou, H.I.
    1956   *A History of Education in Antiquity* (New York: Sheed & Ward).
Newsome, J.D.
    1992   *Greeks, Romans, Jews: Currents of Culture and Belief in the New Testament World*
            (Philadelphia: Trinity Press International).
Nickelsburg, G.W.E.
    1981   *Jewish Literature Between the Bible and the Mishnah* (Philadelphia: Fortress Press).
Norden, E.
    1923   *Die antike Kunstprosa vom VI. Jahrhundert v. Chr. bis in die Zeit der Renaissance*
            (Leipzig).
O'Hagan, A.
    1974   'The Martyr in the Fourth Book of Maccabees', *SBFLA* 24: 94-120.
Obermann, J.
    1931   'The Sepulchre of the Maccabean Martyrs', *JBL* 50: 250-65.
Perler, O.
    1949   'Das vierte Makkabäerbuch, Ignatius von Antiochien und die ältesten Mar-
            tyrerberichte', *RAC* 25: 47-72.
Pfeiffer, R.H.
    1949   *History of New Testament Times, with an Introduction to the Apocrypha* (New
            York: Harper & Brothers).
Pfitzner, V.C.
    1967   *Paul and the Agon Motif: Traditional Athletic Imagery in the Pauline Literature* (Lei-
            den: E.J. Brill).
Rahlfs, A.
    1935   *Septuaginta* (Stuttgart: Deutsche Bibelgesellschaft).
Redditt, P.D.
    1983   'The Concept of *Nomos* in Fourth Maccabees', *CBQ* 45: 249-70.
Renehan, R.
    1972   'The Greek Philosophic Background of Fourth Maccabees', *Rheinisches
            Museum für Philologie* 115: 223-38.
Robbins, V.K.
    1993   'Rhetoric and Culture: Exploring Types of Cultural Rhetoric in a Text', in
            S.E. Porter and T.H. Olbricht (eds.), *Rhetoric and the New Testament*
            (JSNTSup, 90; Sheffield: JSOT Press): 447-67.
Rost, L.
    1971   *Einleitung in die alttestamentlichen Apokryphen und Pseudepigraphen* (Heidelberg:
            Quelle & Meyer)
Russell, D.S.
    1972   *Between the Testaments* (Philadelphia: Fortress Press).
de Ste Croix, G.E.M.
    1954   'Suffragium: From Vote to Patronage', *British Journal of Sociology* 5: 33-48.

Saller, R.P.
    1982   *Personal Patronage under the Early Empire* (Cambridge: Cambridge University
            Press).
Schatkin, M.
    1974   'The Maccbean Martyrs', *VC* 28: 97-113.
Schürer, E.
    1986   *The History of the Jewish People in the Age of Jesus Christ (175 BC–AD 135): A
            New English Version*, I (ed. Geza Vermes, Fergus Millar and Martin Goodman;
            3 vols., Edinburgh: T. & T. Clark).
Seeley, D.
    1990   *The Noble Death: Graeco-Roman Martyrology and Paul's Concept of Salvation*
            (JSNTSup, 28; Sheffield: Sheffield Academic Press).
Smallwood, M.
    1981   *The Jews Under Roman Rule* (Leiden: E.J. Brill).
Staniforth, M.
    1964   *Meditations of Marcus Aurelius* (Harmondsworth: Penguin Books).
    1968   *Early Christian Writings: The Apostolic Fathers* (London: Penguin Books).
Staples, P.
    1966   'The Unused Lever? A Study on the Possible Literary Influence of the Greek
            Maccabean Literature in the New Testament', *Modern Churchman* 9: 218-24.
Swete, H.B.
    1894   *The Old Testament in Greek*. (Cambridge: Cambridge University Press) III.
Tcherikover, V.
    1961   *Hellenistic Civilization and the Jews* (Philadelphia: Jewish Publication Society of
            America).
Thyen, H.
    1955   *Der Stil der jüdische-hellenistichen Homilie* (Göttingen: Vandenhoeck & Ruprecht).
Torrey, C.C.
    1945   *The Apocryphal Literature: A Brief Introduction* (New Haven: Yale University
            Press).
Townshend, R.B.
    1913   'The Fourth Book of Maccabees', in R.H. Charles (ed.), *The Apocrypha and
            Pseudepigrapha of the Old Testament* (Oxford: Clarendon Press) II: 653-85.
van Henten, J.W.
    1986   'Datierung und Herkunft des Vierten Makkabäerbuches', in J.W. van Henten,
            H.J. de Jonge *et al.* (eds.), *Tradition and Re-interpretation in Jewish and Early
            Christian Literature* (Leiden: E.J. Brill): 136-49.
    1993   'The Tradition-Historical Background of Romans 3.25: A Search for Pagan
            and Jewish Parallels', in M.C. De Boer (ed.), *From Jesus to John: Essays on Jesus
            and New Testament Christology in Honor of Marinus de Jonge* (JSNTSup, 84;
            Sheffield: Sheffield Academic Press): 101-28.
    1994   'A Jewish Epitaph in a Literary Text: 4 Macc 17.8-10', in J.W. van Henten
            and P.W. van der Horst (eds.), *Studies in Early Jewish Epigraphy* (AGJU, 21;
            Leiden: E.J. Brill): 44-69.
    1995   'The Martyrs as Heroes of the Christian People', in M. Lamberigts and P. van
            Deun (eds.), *Martyrium in Multidisciplinary Perspective* (Leuven: Leuven Univer-
            sity Press): 303-22.

Williams, D. S.
  1987   'Josephus and the Authorship of IV Maccabees: A Critical Investigation' (PhD
          Dissertation, Hebrew Union College).
Williams, S.K.
  1975   *Jesus' Death as Saving Event: The Background and Origin of a Concept* (HTRDS,
          2; Missoula, MT: Scholars Press).
Winslow, D.F.
  1974   'The Maccabean Martyrs: Early Christian Attitudes', *Judaism* 23: 78-86.

INDEXES

INDEX OF REFERENCES

OLD TESTAMENT

New Testament

PSEUDEPIGRAPHA

CLASSICAL REFERENCES

OTHER ANCIENT REFERENCES

INDEX OF AUTHORS

Tarzana

The Curry Bowl

Gregson & Kathrine
Carson
) 3 5 (?)

210

134 → 101

Los Virginas Rd
   Left at ramp

Turns into Malibu Canyon Rd

At "T", turn left to Surfer's Beach

on right to Zuma Beach (larger,
                    more open)